Anonymous

College hymnal

A selection of Christian praise-songs for the uses of worship in universities, colleges

and advanced schools

Anonymous

College hymnal
A selection of Christian praise-songs for the uses of worship in universities, colleges and advanced schools

ISBN/EAN: 9783337266295

Printed in Europe, USA, Canada, Australia, Japan

Cover: Foto ©Thomas Meinert / pixelio.de

More available books at **www.hansebooks.com**

COLLEGE
HYMNAL

A Selection of Christian
Praise-Songs for the uses
of Worship in Universities
Colleges and Advanced
Schools

New York and Chicago
THE BIGLOW & MAIN COMPANY
1897

GUNTHER & COMPANY,
Music Typographers, 63 Duane St., N. Y.

THIS selection has been prepared with equal consideration for vitality and usefulness in the words, and for vigor and breadth in the music to which these are set.

As to the hymns they are first of all frankly and fervently Christian. Those have been chosen which are both distinctly lyrical in form and earnestly devout in substance, appropriate to voice the sincere feelings and purposes of youth, virile with its wholesome and hopeful courage, and uttering that spirit of direct and genuine praise, which however serious and deep is never morbid or artificial.

The tunes have been chosen upon careful reflection and comparison, under the tests of just such use as that for which this Hymnal is designed. They have individuality, animation, and durable interest. The more part of them are already well-endeared, and such as are new to some will, under thoughtful song, reward the effort they invite. There are no measures here without robust character and movement. Every number is adapted to the service of hearty praise, and whether tender or triumphant, calm or grand, strong melody is interwoven with pure and noble harmony upon every page.

In every case the hymn is meant to be sung to the tune just preceding. The typography and form of the book, with its large print and convenient weight, may be left to commend themselves. That it may promote a more ardent and satisfactory attention to the high ends of worship, and become an inspiration and a joy to many eager groups of American collegians, is the hope, as it has been the incitement, of the compiler.

M. W. S.

ORDER OF HYMNS

According to their general Subjects and Numbers.

College Hymnal

1

Meet and right it is to sing.

7s & 6s P.
CHARLES WESLEY, 1749. *Abr.*

" With joy shall ye draw water out of the wells of salvation."

Excelsius.
JOHN H. CORNELL, 1872.

1. MEET and right it is to sing, In ev - ery time and place, Glo - ry to our heavenly King,—The God of truth and grace; Join we, then, with sweet ac - cord, All in one thanksgiv - ing join;— Ho - ly, ho - ly, ho - ly Lord! E - ter - nal praise be Thine.

By permission of E. & J. B. Young & Co.

2 Thee the first-born sons of light,
    In choral symphonies,
Praise by day, day without night,
    And never, never cease.
Angels, and archangels, all
    Praise the mystic Three in One,
Sing, and stop, and gaze, and fall,
    O'erwhelmed, before Thy throne!

2   God of the morning! at whose voice.

L. M.   *" The Lord thinketh on me."*   **Luton.**

Isaac Watts, 17-9.   George Burder, 1770.

1. God of the morn-ing! at whose voice The cheer-ful Sun makes haste to rise,

And like a gi - ant doth re - joice, To run his jour - ney thro the skies.

2 Oh! like the Sun, may I fulfill
Th' appointed duties of the day;
With ready mind, and active will,
March on, and keep my heavenly way.

3 But I shall rove and lose the race,
If God, my Sun, shall disappear,
And leave me in the world's wide maze
To follow every wandering star.

4 Lord! Thy commands are clean and pure,
Enlightening our beclouded eyes;
Thy threatenings just, Thy promise sure,
Thy gospel makes the simple wise.

5 Give me Thy counsel for my guide,
And then receive me to Thy bliss;
All my desires and hopes beside
Are faint, and cold, compared with this.

3

1 Again as evening's shadow falls,
We gather in these hallowed walls,
And vesper hymn and vesper prayer
Rise mingling on the holy air.

2 May struggling hearts that seek release
Here find the rest of God's own peace,
And strengthened here by hymn and prayer,
Lay down the burden and the care.

3 O God, our Light, to Thee we bow;
Within all shadows standest Thou.
Give deeper calm than night can bring,
Give sweeter songs than lips can sing.

4 Life's tumult we must meet again,
We cannot at the shrine remain:
But in the spirit's secret cell
May hymn and prayer forever dwell.

Samuel Longfellow, 1859.

4 Hues of the rich unfolding morn.

L. M. *" Bring your sacrifices every morning."* **Duke Street.**

JOHN KEBLE, 1827. *Abr.* JOHN HATTON, 1790.

1. HUES of the rich un - fold - ing morn, That ere the glo - rious sun be born,

By some soft touch in - vis - i - ble A - round his path are taught to swell!

2 Oh, timely happy, timely wise
Hearts that with rising morn arise!
Eyes that the beam celestial view,
Which evermore makes all things new.

3 New every morning is the Love
Our wak'ning and uprising prove,—
Thro sleep and darkness safely brought,
Restored to life and power and thought.

4 New mercies, each returning day,
Hover around us while we pray,
New perils past, new sins forgiven,
New thoughts of God, new hopes of Heaven.

5 If, on our daily course, our mind
Be set to hallow all we find,
New treasures still, of countless price,
God will provide for sacrifice.

6 Old friends, old scenes, will lovelier be,
As more of Heaven in each we see;
Some softening gleam of love and prayer,
Shall dawn on every cross and care.

7 Oh could we learn that sacrifice,
What lights would all around us rise!
How would our hearts with wisdom talk
Along Life's dullest dreariest walk!

8 The trivial round, the common task,
Would furnish all we ought to ask,
Room to deny ourselves, a road
To bring us daily nearer God.

9 Only, O Lord, in Thy dear love
Fit us for perfect rest above,
And help us, this and every day,
To live more nearly as we pray.

5 All praise to Thee, my God, this night.

L. M. *"Thou mak'st the outgoings of the morning and evening to rejoice."* **Tallis' Canon.**

Thomas Ken, 1697. *Abr.*   Thomas Tallis, 1560. *Har.*

1. All praise to Thee, my God! this night, For all the bless-ings of the light.

Keep me, oh, keep me, King of kings! Be-neath Thine own al-might-y wings.

2 Forgive me, Lord, for Thy dear Son,
The ill that I this day have done;
That with the world, myself, and Thee,
I, ere I sleep, at peace may be.

3 When in the night I sleepless lie,
My soul with heavenly thoughts supply!
Let no ill dreams disturb my rest,
No powers of darkness me molest.

4 Oh! may my soul on Thee repose,
And may sweet sleep mine eye lids close,—
Sleep that may me more vigorous make,
To serve my God, when I awake.

5 Teach me to live, that I may dread
The grave as little as my bed;
Teach me to die, that so I may
Rise, glorious, at the awful day.

6

1 Awake, my soul, and with the Sun
Thy daily stage of duty run,
Shake off dull sloth, and joyful rise
To pay thy morning sacrifice!

2 Wake and lift up thyself, my heart,
And with the angels bear thy part,
Who all night long unwearied sing
High praise to their eternal King!

3 Lord, I my vows to Thee renew;
Disperse my sins as morning dew,
Guard my first springs of thought and will,
And with Thyself my spirit fill.   [will,

4 Direct, control, suggest this day
All I design, or do, or say,
That all my powers, with all their might,
In Thy sole glory may unite.

Thomas Ken, 1697. *Abr.*

7 **Blest angels, while we silent lie.**

L. M.   "*He turneth the shadow of death into the morning.*"   Anglican.

THOMAS KEN, 1697. *Abr.*   EDWIN GEORGE MONK, 1867.

1. BLEST an - gels, while we si - lent lie, Ye al - le - lu - ias sing on high,

Ye joy - ful hymn the Ev - er - Blest Be - fore the throne and nev - er rest.

8

2 I with your choir celestial join,
In offering up a hymn divine,
With you in Heaven I hope to dwell
And bid the night and world farewell.

3 Lord, lest the tempter me surprise,
Watch over Thine own sacrifice!
All loose, all idle thoughts cast out,
And make my very dreams devout.

4 Shine on me, Lord, new life impart,
Pure ardors kindle in my heart;
One ray of Thine all-quick'ning light
Dispels the sloth and clouds of night.

5 All praise to Thee, in light arrayed,
Who light Thy dwelling-place hast made!
A boundless ocean of bright beams
From Thine all-glorious Godhead streams.

1 Now with Creation's morning song
Let us, as children of the day,
With wakened heart and purpose strong,
The works of darkness cast away!

2 Oh! may the morn, so pure, so clear,
Its own sweet calm in us instil;—
A guileless mind, a heart sincere,
Simplicity of word and will.

3 And ever, as the day glides by,
May we the busy senses rein;
Keep guard upon the hand and eye,
Nor let the conscience suffer stain.

4 Grant us, O God! in love to Thee,
Clear eyes to measure things below,
Faith the invisible to see,
And wisdom Thee in all to know.

Lat. Tr. EDWARD CASWALL, 1848.
Alt. SAMUEL LONGFELLOW, 1864.

9   Abide with me! fast falls the eventide.

10. 10. 10. 10.   " *Until the day break, and the shadows flee away.*"   Eventide.

Henry F. Lyte, 1847. Abr.   William H. Monk, 1860.

Adagio.

1. A-BIDE with me! fast falls the e - ven - tide; The dark-ness deep-ens; Lord, with me a - bide!

When oth - er help-ers fail, and comforts flee, Help of the helpless, Oh, a - bide with me! A - men.

2 Swift to its close ebbs out life's little day;
  Earth's joys grow dim, its glories pass away;
  Change and decay in all around I see;
  O Thou, Who changest not, abide with me.

3 Thou on my head in early youth didst smile;
  And, tho rebellious and perverse meanwhile,
  Thou hast not left me, oft as I left Thee;—
  On to the close, O Lord, abide with me.

4 I need Thy presence every passing hour;
  What but Thy grace can foil the Tempter's power?
  Who, like Thyself, my guide and stay can be?
  Thro cloud and sunshine, Lord, abide with me.

5 Not a brief glance I beg, a passing word:
  But as Thou dwell'st with Thy disciples, Lord,
  Familiar, condescending, patient, free;
  Come, not to sojourn but abide with me!

6 Hold Thou Thy Cross before my closing eyes;
  Shine thro the gloom, and point me to the skies.
  Heaven's morning breaks! and Earth's vain shadows flee;
  In life, in death, O Lord, abide with me. *Amen.*

10 Holy, Holy, Holy! Lord God Almighty.

12.12.12.10. *" Glorious in holiness, fearful in praises."* **Nicœa.**

REGINALD HEBER, 1819. JOHN B. DYKES, 1861.

1. Ho-LY, holy! ho-ly, Lord God Al-might-y! Ear-ly in the morning our song shall rise to Thee;

Ho-ly, ho-ly, holy, Mer-ci-ful and Might-y! God in Three Per-sons, bless-ed Trin-i-ty!

2 Holy, holy, holy! all the saints adore Thee,
   Casting down their golden crowns around the glassy sea;
   Cherubim and Seraphim falling down before Thee,
   Which wert, and art, and evermore shalt be.

3 Holy, holy, holy! tho the darkness hide Thee,
   Tho the eye of sinful man Thy glory may not see,
   Only Thou art holy; there is none beside Thee,
   Perfect in power, in love, and purity.

4 Holy, holy, holy! Lord God Almighty!
   All Thy works shall praise Thy name, in Earth, and sky, and sea.
   Holy, holy, holy! Merciful and Mighty!
   God in Three Persons, blessèd Trinity!

11 The radiant morn hath past away.

8.8.8.4.   *" He knoweth them that put their trust in Him."*   **Redcliff.**

GODFREY THRING, 1866.   EDWARD JOHN HOPKINS, 1863. *Alt.*

1. THE radiant morn hath past a - way, And spent too soon her gold-en store, The shadows of de -

part - ing day, Creep on once more.

2 Our life is but an autumn day,
Its glorious noon how quickly past!
Lead us, O Christ, Thou Living Way,
Safe home at last.

3 Oh! by Thy soul-inspiring grace,
Uplift our hearts to realms on high;
Help us to look to that bright place
Beyond the sky;—

4 Where light and life and joy and peace
In undivided empire reign
And thronging angels never cease
Their deathless strain;—

5 Where saints are clothed in spotless
white,
And evening shadows never fall,
Where Thou, Eternal Light of Light!
Art Lord of all.

12 Softly now the light of day.

7.7.7.7.   *" An inheritance * * that fadeth not."*   **Esther.**

GEORGE W. DOANE, 1824. *Abr.*   JOSEPH BARNBY, 1878.

1. SOFT - LY now the light of day Fades up - on my sight a - way; Free from care, from

Morning and Evening.

la-bor free, Lord! I would commune with Thee.

2 Thou, whose all-pervading eye
Naught escapes, without, within!
Pardon each infirmity,
Open fault, and secret sin.

3 Soon, for me, the light of day
Shall for ever pass away;
Then, from sin and sorrow free,
Take me, Lord! to dwell with Thee.

13 'Tis gone, that bright and orbèd blaze.

L. M. " The Lord God is a sun and a shield." **Hursley.**

JOHN KEBLE, 1827. Abr. PETER RITTER, 1792. Arr.

1. 'Tis gone, that bright and orb - ed blaze, Fast fad - ing from our wist - ful gaze;

Yon man-tling cloud has hid from sight The last faint pulse of quiv - 'ring light.

2 Sun of my soul, Thou Saviour dear,
It is not night if Thou be near:
Oh, may no Earth-born cloud arise
To hide Thee from Thy servant's eyes.

3 When with dear friends sweet talk I hold,
And all the flowers of life unfold;
Let not my heart within me burn
Except in all I Thee discern.

4 Abide with me from morn till eve;
For without Thee I cannot live.
Abide with me when night is nigh;
For without Thee I dare not die.

5 Come near and bless us when we wake,
Ere thro the world our way we take,
Till in the ocean of Thy love
We lose ourselves in Heaven above.

14   The day is gently sinking to a close.

10.10.10.10.10.10.   *"Not put in fear by any terror."*   **Sunset Chant.**

CHRISTOPHER WORDSWORTH, 1862.   JOSEPH BARNBY, 1880.

1. The day is gently... sink-ing to a close, Fainter, and yet more faint, the sun-light glows.

O brightness of Thy Father's glo - ry, Thou, E - ter - nal Light of Light! be with us now.

Where Thou art present, darkness can-not be. Midnight is glorious noon, O Lord, with Thee. A-men.

2 Thou, who in darkness | walking didst appear |
Upon the waves, and | Thy disciples cheer, ‖
Come, Lord, in lonesome | days, when storms assail, |
And earthly hopes and human succors fail; ‖
When all is dark, may | we behold Thee nigh, |
And hear Thy | voice, *"Fear not, for it is I."* ‖

3 The weary world is | mouldering to decay, ‖
Its glories wane, its | pageants fade away; ‖

Morning and Evening.

In that last sunset, | when the stars shall fall, ||
May we arise, awakened by Thy call, ||
With Thee, O Lord, for | ever to abide, ||
In that blest | day which has no eventide! || *Amen.*

15   Upraised from sleep, to Thee we kneel.

" He that keepeth thee will not slumber."

12.8.8.4.4.7.

ANCIENT GREEK HYMN, *Cir.* 300 A.D.
Tr. ROBERT C. SINGLETON, 1872, *Abr.*

Matin Hymn.

JOSEPH BARNBY, 1872.

1. UP - RAISED from sleep, to Thee we kneel, as day doth break. To
Thee, O Lord, a - loud we sing, To Thee the song of an - gels bring; For
mer - cy's sake, Oh, pit - y take, O ho - ly, ho - ly, ho - ly! A - men.

2 Thou, Lord, hast from my couch of rest uplifted me;
Oh, light my mind, Oh, light my heart,
And ope my lips to take their part
In praising Thee, Blest Trinity!
O holy, holy, holy! *Amen.*

16 God that madest Earth and Heaven.

8.4.8.4.8.8.8.4.   *" The darkness and the light are both alike."*   Temple.

Stanza 1. REGINALD HEBER, 1827.
Stanza 2, RICHARD WHATELY, 1860.

EDWARD J. HOPKINS, 1867.

1. God, that mad - est Earth and Heav - en, Dark - ness and light; Who the day for
toil hast giv - en, For rest the night; May Thine an - gel guards de - fend us! Slum - ber
sweet Thy mer - cy send us! Ho - ly dreams and hopes at - tend us, This live-long night!

2 Guard us waking, guard us sleeping,
    And when we die,
May we, in Thy mighty keeping,
    All peaceful lie.
When the last dread call shall wake us,
Do not Thou, our God, forsake us:
But to reign in glory take us
    With Thee on high.

17 The shadows of the evening hours.

C. M. D.   *" Even the night shall be light about me."*   **St. Leonard.**

ADELAIDE ANNE PROCTER, 1858. *Abr.*   HENRY HILES, 1870.

1. THE shad - ows of the eve-ning hours Fall from the dark'ning sky. Up - on the fragrance of the flow'rs The dews of eve - ning lie. Be - fore Thy throne, O Lord of Heav'n! We kneel at close of day; Look on Thy children from on high, And hear us while we pray.

2 Slowly the rays of daylight fade;
  So fade within the heart
The hopes in earthly love and joy
  That, one by one, depart.
The brightness of the coming night
  Upon the darkness rolls;
With hopes of future glory chase
  The shadows from our souls.

3 Let Thine unworldly peace, O Lord,
  Upon our souls descend,
From midnight fears and perils Thou
  Our trembling hearts defend.
Give us a respite from our toil,
  Calm and subdue our woes.
Thro the long day we suffer, Lord,—
  Oh, give us now repose.

18 Thou glorious Sun of Righteousness!

L. M. *" The glory of the God of Israel came from the way of the east."* **Angels.**
CHARLOTTE ELLIOTT, 1839. *Abr.*   ORLANDO GIBBONS, 1614.

1. Thou glo-rious Sun of Right-cous-ness! On this day ris'n to set no more!

Shine on me now to heal, to bless, With bright-er beams than e'er be-fore.

19

2 Shine on Thy work of grace within,
   On each celestial blossom there;
   Destroy each bitter root of sin,
   And make Thy garden new and fair.

3 Shine on Thy pure eternal word,
   Its mysteries to my soul reveal;
   And whether read, remembered, heard,
   Oh, let it quicken, strengthen, heal!

4 Shine on those unseen things displayed
   To faith's far-penetrating eye;
   And let their splendor cast a shade
   On every earthly vanity.

5 Shine, till Thy glorious beams shall chase
   The blinding film from every eye;
   Till every earthly dwelling-place
   Shall hail the Dayspring from on high!

1 HERE let Thy holy days be kept;
   And be this place to worship given,
   Like that bright spot where Jacob slept,
   The house of God, the gate of Heaven.

2 Here may Thine honor dwell; and here,
   As incense, let Thy children's prayer,
   From contrite hearts and lips sincere,
   Rise on the still and holy air.

3 Here be Thy praise devoutly sung;
   Here let Thy truth beam forth to save,
   As when of old Thy Spirit hung,
   On wings of light, o'er Jordan's wave.

4 And when the lips, that with Thy name
   Are vocal now, to dust shall turn,
   On others may devotion's flame
   Be kindled here, and purely burn!
   JOHN PIERPONT, 1823. *Abr.*

20 Hail, thou bright and sacred morn.

7.7.7.7.7.7.   *"The light of the gospel of the glory of Christ."*   **Dies Christi.**

JULIA ANNE ELLIOTT, 1835. *Abr.*   JOSEPH BARNBY, 1880.

1. Hail, thou bright and sa - cred morn, Ris'n with glad - ness in thy beams!

Light, which not of Earth is born, From thy dawn in glo - ry streams.

Airs of Heav'n are breath'd a - round, And each place is ho - - ly ground.

2 Great Creator! Who, this day,
  From Thy perfect work didst rest;
  By the souls that own Thy sway
    Hallow'd be its hours and blest;
  Cares of Earth aside be thrown,
  This day giv'n to Heaven alone.

3 Saviour! who, this day, didst break
  The dark prison of the tomb,
  Bid my slumbering soul awake;

Shine thro all its sin and gloom.
Let me, from my bonds set free,
Rise from sin, and live to Thee.

4 Blessèd Spirit! Comforter!
  Sent, this day, from Christ on high,
  Lord, on me Thy gifts confer,
    Cleanse, illumine, sanctify!
  All Thine influence shed abroad;
  Lead me to the truth of God!

21   Early, my God! without delay.

C. M.
ISAAC WATTS, 1719. *Abr.*

"The way of man is not in himself."

Lanesboro.
WILLIAM DIXON, 1790.

1. Ear-ly, my God! with-out de - lay, I haste to seek Thy face; My thirst-y spir - it

faints a - way,—My thirst - y spir - it faints a - way,—With-out Thy cheer-ing grace.

2 So pilgrims on the scorching sand,
  Beneath a burning sky,
Long for a cooling stream at hand,
  And they must drink or die.

3 I've seen Thy glory and Thy power
  Thro all Thy temple shine;
My God! repeat that heavenly hour,
  That vision so divine.

4 Not life itself, with all its joys,
  Can my best passions move;
Or raise so high my cheerful voice,
  As Thy forgiving love.

5 Thus, till my last expiring day,
  I'll bless my God and King;
Thus will I lift my hands to pray,
  And tune my lips to sing.

22   Let every mortal ear attend.

C. M.
ISAAC WATTS, 1707. *Abr.*

"The mirage shall become a pool."

Warwick.
SAMUEL STANLEY, 1800.

1. Let ev - ery mor - tal ear at - tend, And ev - ery heart re - joice!

The Lord's House.

The trum-pet of the gos-pel sounds With an in - - vit - ing voice.

2 Rivers of love and mercy here,
   In a rich ocean join.
Salvation in abundance flows,
   Like floods of milk and wine.

3 Dear God! the treasures of Thy love
   Are everlasting mines,
Deep as our helpless miseries are,
   And boundless as our sins!

4 The happy gates of gospel grace
   Stand open night and day.
Lord, we are come to seek supplies,
   And drive our wants away.

23

1 Now that the day-star glimmers bright,
   We suppliantly pray
That He, the uncreated Light,
   May guide us on our way.

2 No sinful word, nor deed of wrong,
   Nor thoughts that idly rove,
But simple truth be on our tongue,
   And in our hearts be love.

3 And grant that to Thine honor, Lord,
   Our daily toil may tend;
That we begin it at Thy word,
   And in Thy favor end.

Lat. tr. JOHN HENRY NEWMAN, 1842. *Abr.*

24   We close Thy blessèd word.

6.6.6.6.   "*That we may lead a tranquil and quiet life in all godliness and gravity.*"   **Moseley.**
M. W. S. 1887.   HENRY SMART, 1878.

1 We close Thy blessed word, Where pow'r and promise meet, What faith with rapture heard May blameless lives complete.

2 Here hath heartsickness learned
   Who makes the sad to sing,
And strife-tossed reason turned
   To love unquestioning.

3 Receive our twilight hymn,
   Take, Lord, our evening prayer;

Our souls, while day grows dim,
   Surrender to Thy care.

4 Home to their fold, Thy breast,
   Thy sheep return once more.
Thou, who dost guide to rest,
   Thyself shalt guard the door.

𝕮𝖍𝖊 𝕷𝖔𝖗𝖉'𝖘 𝕳𝖔𝖚𝖘𝖊.

25   Pleasant are Thy courts above.

7s, D.   *"How aimiable are Thy tabernacles."*   **Maidstone.**

HENRY F. LYTE, 1834. *Abr.*   WALTER B. GILBERT, 1862.

1. { Pleas - ant are Thy courts a - bove, In the land of light and love ; }
   { Pleas - ant are Thy courts be - low, In this land of sin and woe. }

Oh, my spir - it longs and faints For the con - verse of Thy saints,

For the bright - ness of Thy face, King of glo - ry, God of grace.

2 Happy souls! their praises flow
Ever in this vale of woe ;
Waters in the desert rise,
Manna feeds them from the skies.
On they go from strength to strength,
Till they reach Thy throne at length ;
At Thy feet adoring fall,
Who hast led them safe thro all.

3 Lord, be mine this prize to win ;
Guide me thro a world of sin ;
Keep me by Thy saving grace.
Give me at Thy side a place.
Sun and shield alike Thou art,
Guide and guard my erring heart ;
Grace and glory flow from Thee,
Shower, oh shower them, Lord, on me.

26 Saviour, again to Thy dear name.

"The peace of God, which passeth all understanding, shall guard your thoughts and your hearts in Christ Jesus."

10.10.10.10.

JOHN ELLERTON, 1866. *Abr.*

Pax Dei.

EDWARD J. HOPKINS, 1866.

1. SAV - IOUR, a - gain to Thy dear Name we raise, With one ac -
cord, our part - ing hymn of praise. We stand to bless Thee ere our
wor - ship cease, Then, low - ly bend - ing, wait Thy word of peace. A - men.

2 Grant us Thy peace upon our homeward way;
With Thee began, with Thee shall end the day.
Guard Thou the lips from sin, the hearts from shame,
That in this house have called upon Thy Name.

3 Grant us Thy peace, Lord, thro the coming night,
Turn Thou for us i s darkness into light;
From harm and danger keep Thy children free,
For dark and light are both alike to Thee. *Amen.*

27 The day of praise is done.

S. M.

"*He is thy praise, and He is thy God.*"

Leighton.

JOHN ELLERTON, 1867. *Abr.*

HENRY W. GREATOREX, 1849.

1. THE day of praise is done, The eve - ning shad - ows fall;

Yet pass not from us with the Sun, True Light that light - 'nest all!

2 Around Thy throne on high,
Where night can never be,
The white-robed harpers of the sky
Bring ceaseless hymns to Thee.

3 Too faint our anthems here,
Too soon of praise we tire:
But oh, the strains how full and clear
Of that eternal choir!

4 Yet, Lord! to Thy dear will
If Thou attune the heart,
We in Thine angels' music still
May bear our lower part.

5 Shine Thou within us then,
A day that knows no end,
Till songs of angels and of men
In perfect praise shall blend.

28 Stand up, and bless the Lord.

S. M.

"*A holy priesthood, to offer up spiritual sacrifices.*"

Silver Street.

JAMES MONTGOMERY, 1825. *Abr.*

ISAAC SMITH, 1770.

Marcato.

1. STAND up, and bless the Lord, Ye peo - ple _ of His choice:

The Lord's House.

Stand up, and bless the Lord, your God, With heart, and soul, and voice.

2 Oh, for the living flame,
  From His own altar brought,
To touch our lips, our minds inspire,
  And wing to Heaven our thought.

3 Tho high above all praise,
  Above all blessing high,
Who would not fear His holy name,
  And laud and magnify?

4 God is our strength and song,
  And His salvation ours;
Then be His love in Christ proclaimed
  With all our ransomed powers.

5 Stand up, and bless the Lord,
  The Lord your God adore;
Stand up, and bless His glorious Name,
  Henceforth for evermore.

29 Heavenly Father, Sovereign Lord.

7.7.7.7.
" Ye that seek after God, let your heart live."

Eli.

BENJAMIN WILLIAMS, 1778. Alt.

MICHAEL COSTA, 1855.

1. HEAVENLY Father, Sovereign Lord,
Be Thy glorious name adored!
Lord, Thy mercies never fail;
Hail, ce·les · tial goodness, hail!

2 Tho unworthy, Lord, Thine ear,
  Deign our humble songs to hear;
Purer praise we hope to bring,
  When around Thy throne we sing.

3 While on Earth ordained to stay,
  Guide our footsteps in Thy way,

Till we come to dwell with Thee,
Till we all Thy glory see.

4 Then, with angel-harps again,
  We will wake a nobler strain;
There, in joyful songs of praise,
  Our triumphant voices raise.

30

Lord of the worlds above.

"Thou shalt rejoice before the Lord thy God in all that Thou puttest thine hand unto."

6.6.6.6.8.8.

ISAAC WATTS, 1719.

St. Godric.

JOHN B. DYKES, 1861.

1. Lord of the worlds a - bove, How pleasant and how fair   The dwellings of Thy love, Thine

earth-ly temples are !   To Thine a-bode my heart aspires, With warm desires to see my God.

2 Oh! happy souls who pray,
  Where God appoints to hear!
Oh! happy men who pay
  Their constant service there!
They praise Thee still; and happy they,
Who love the way to Zion's hill.

3 They go from strength to strength,
  Thro this dark vale of tears,
Till each arrives at length,
  Till each in Heaven appears;
Oh! glorious seat, when God our King,
Shall thither bring our willing feet.

31

This is the day of Light.

S. M.

JOHN ELLERTON, 1867. Abr.

"A morning without clouds."

Olmutz.

The Eighth Gregorian Tone, 500.
Adap. LOWELL MASON, 1 24.

1. This is the day of Light! Let there be light to - day! O Day-spring, rise up-

on our night, And chase its gloom a - way.

2 This is the day of Peace !
Thy peace our spirits fill ;
Bid Thou the blasts of discord cease,
The waves of strife be still.

3 This is the day of Prayer !
Let Earth to Heaven draw near ;
Lift up our hearts to seek Thee there;
Come down to meet us here.

32 See the clouds upon the mountains.

Under His feet as it were a paved work of sapphire stone, and as it were the very heaven for clearness.

8.7.8.7.7.7.
WILLIAM B. COLLYER, 1837. *Alt.*

Ilkley.
JAMES W. ELLIOTT.

1. SEE the clouds up - on the mount-ains, Roll - ing, ris- ing, melt a - way, Light, forth flowing from its

fountains, Pours an unobstruct-ed ray. Lord, may ev-ery shadow fly From my soul, before Thine eye.

2 Rise, my soul, the day is breaking,
Gladdened nature drinks the light ;
From the sleep of darkness waking,
Put off all the clouds of night.
In the beauty of His grace
Lift to God thy thankful face.

3 Take the rest this day is bringing,
Best of all our earthly days,
Enter thou His gates with singing,
Tread the hallowed floor with praise.
In the radiance of His love
Yield thy heart to God above.

33   O day of rest and gladness.

"O satisfy us in the morning with Thy mercy; that we may rejoice and be glad all our days."

7s & 6s, D.

Christopher Wordsworth, 1858. *Abr.*

St. Anselm.

Joseph Barnby, 1868.

1. O DAY of rest and glad-ness, O day of joy and light! O balm of care and sad-ness, Most beau-ti-ful, most bright! On thee, the high and low-ly, Thro a-ges joined in tune Sing, "Ho-ly! ho-ly! ho-ly!"To the great God Tri-une.

2 Thou art a port, protected
From storms that round us rise;
A garden, intersected
With streams of Paradise;
Thou art a cooling fountain,
In life's dry, dreary sand;
From thee, like Pisgah's mountain,
We view our promised land.

3 To-day on weary nations
The heavenly manna falls;
To holy convocations
The silver trumpet calls.
A day of sweet reflection
Thou art, a day of love,
A day of resurrection
From Earth to things above.

34   Praise the Lord! ye heavens, adore Him!

8s & 7s, D.   *" We will walk in the name of Jehovah, our God, forever and ever."*   **Oratorio.**

ANON, 1796.   GEORGE F. LE JEUNE, 1872.

1. PRAISE the Lord! ye heav'ns, a - dore Him, Praise Him, an-gels   in   the height! Sun and Moon, re -

joice be-fore Him, Praise Him, all ye stars of light! Praise the Lord; for He   hath spo-ken,—Worlds His

might-y   voice o - beyed. Laws which nev - er   shall be bro-ken For their guidance He hath made.

Used by permission.

2 Praise the Lord! for He is glorious,
     Never shall His promise fail.
God hath made His saints victorious,
     Sin and death shall not prevail.
Praise the God of our salvation,
     Hosts on high His power proclaim;
Heaven and Earth and all Creation,
     Laud and magnify His name.

35 I will extol Thee every day.

C. M.
"*To Him shalt thou cleave, and by His name shalt thou swear.*"
Burlington.

THOMAS MACKELLAR, 1871. *Abr.*

JOHN F. BURROWES, 1830.

1. I WILL ex - tol Thee ev - ery day, My God, O glo - rious King;

And I will bless Thy name for aye, Thy praise for - ev - er sing.

2 One generation, praising Thee,
Shall testimony bear
Unto the next, and wond'ringly
Thy mighty acts declare.

3 The Lord our God is good to all;
For all are in His thought,
His tender mercies richly fall
On all that He hath wrought.

4 Thou openest Thy hand of grace,
And Thou dost satisfy
The wants of all in every place
Who for Thy presence cry.

5 My mouth shall joyfully proclaim
His praise from day to day.
Let all flesh bless His holy name
Forever and for aye!

36

1 Up to those bright and gladsome hills
Whence flows my weal and mirth
I look, and sigh for Him who fills,
Unseen, both Heaven and Earth.

2 He is alone my help and hope
That I shall not be moved;
His watchful eye is ever ope,
And guardeth His beloved.

3 The glorious God is my sole stay,
He is my sun and shade:
The cold by night, the heat by day,
Neither shall me invade.

4 Whether abroad amid the crowd
Or else within my door,
He is my pillar and my cloud,
Now and for evermore.

HENRY VAUGHAN, 1650. *Abr.*

37 There is a book, who runs may read.

C. M.   *" The wise shall understand."*   **Cherith.**

JOHN KEBLE, 1857. *Abr.*   LOUIS SPOHR, 1840.

I. THERE is a book, who runs may read, Which heaven-ly truth im - parts,

And all the lore its schol - ars need, Pure eyes and Chris - tian hearts.

2 The works of God, above, below,
   Within us and around,
Are pages in that book to show
   How God Himself is found.

3 The glorious sky, embracing all,
   Is like the Maker's love,
Wherewith encompassed, great and small
   In peace and order move.

4 Two worlds are ours; 'tis only sin
   Forbids us to descry
The mystic heaven and earth within,
   Plain as the sea and sky.

5 Thou who hast given me eyes to see
   And love this sight so fair,
Give me a heart to find out Thee,
   And read Thee everywhere.

38

1 THE Lord hath builded for Himself,
   He needs no earthly dome;
The universe His dwelling is,
   Eternity His home.

2 Yon glorious sky His temple stands,
   So lofty, bright, and blue,
All lamp'd with stars, and curtain'd round
   With clouds of every hue.

3 Where shall I see Him? How describe
   The dread Eternal One?
His footprints are in every place,
   Himself is found in none.

4 I search the rounds of space and time,
   Nor find His semblance there;
Grandeur has nothing so sublime
   Nor Beauty half so fair.

HENRY F. LYTE, 1833. *Abr.*

39   O Thou whose bounty fills my cup.

C. M.   *" He bore them on His pinions "*   **Lucius.**

JANE FOX CREWDSON, 1860.   GEORGE KINGSLEY, 1853.

1. O Thou whose boun - ty fills my cup With ev - ery bless-ing meet! I give Thee thanks for

ev - ery drop, The bit - ter and the sweet.

3 I thank Thee both for smile and frown
     And for the gain and loss;
I praise Thee for the future crown
     And for the present cross.

4 I thank Thee for the wing of love
     Which stirred my wordly nest,
And for the stormy clouds which drove
     Me fluttering to Thy breast.

2 I praise Thee for the desert road
     And for the river-side,
For all Thy goodness hath bestowed
     And all Thy grace denied.

5 I bless Thee for the glad increase,
     And for the waning joy;
And for this strange, this settled peace,
     Which nothing can destroy.

40   Let us, with a gladsome mind.

7.7.7.7.   *" He bindeth up the waters in His thick cloud, and the cloud is not rent under them."*   **Innocents.**

JOHN MILTON, 1623. *Abr.*   FREDERICK ARTHUR G. OUSELEY, 1867.

1. LET us, with a glad-some mind, Praise the Lord ; for He is kind, For His mer - cies

Praise to God.

aye en-dure, Ev-er faithful, ev-er sure.

2 Let us blaze His name abroad,
For of gods He is the God;
He, with all-commanding might,
Filled the new-made world with light.

3 All things living He doth feed,
His full hand supplies their need;
Let us therefore warble forth
His high majesty and worth.

41   Oh, worship the King!

5.5.5.6, D.   *"His tender mercies are over all His works."*   **Houghton.**

ROBERT GRANT, 1830. *Abr.*   HENRY J. GAUNTLETT, 1860.

1. Oh, worship the King! All-glo-rious a-bove; Oh, grate-ful-ly sing His pow'r and His love!

Our Shield and De-fend-er, The An-cient of Days, Pa-vilioned in splendor, And gird-ed with praise.

2 Thy bountiful care
What tongue can recite?
It breathes in the air,
It shines in the light,
It streams from the hills,
It descends to the plain,
And sweetly distils
In the dew and the rain.

3 Frail children of dust
And feeble as frail,
In Thee do we trust,
Nor find Thee to fail!
Thy mercies how tender,
How firm to the end,
Our Maker, Defender,
Redeemer, and Friend.

42 All people that on Earth do dwell.

L. M.   *"His children shall have a place of refuge."*   **Old Hundredth.**

WILLIAM KETHE, 1561.   The Genevan Psalter.
LOUIS BOURGEOIS, 1554.

1. All peo - ple, that on Earth do dwell, Sing to the Lord with cheer - ful voice,

Him serve with mirth, His praise forth tell, Come ye be - fore Him and re - joice.

2 The Lord, ye know, is God indeed,
  Without our aid He did us make;
  We are His flock, He doth us feed,
  And for His sheep He doth us take.

3 Oh enter then His gates of praise,
  Approach with joy His courts unto;
  Praise, laud, and bless His Name always,
  For it is seemly so to do.

4 For why? the Lord our God is good,
  His mercy is forever sure;
  His truth at all times firmly stood,
  And shall from age to age endure.

43

Praise God, from whom all blessings flow,
Praise Him, all creatures here below!
Praise Him above, ye heavenly host!
Praise Father, Son, and Holy Ghost.
                 THOMAS KEN. 1697.

44

1 We'll crowd Thy gates with thankful songs,
  High as the heavens our voices raise;
  And Earth, with her ten thousand tongues,
  Shall fill Thy courts with sounding praise.

2 Wide as the world is Thy command,
  Vast as eternity Thy love;
  Firm as a rock Thy truth must stand,
  When rolling years shall cease to move.
               ISAAC WATTS, 1719. *Abr.*

45

1 O God! Thou art my God alone;
  Early to Thee my soul shall cry;
  A pilgrim in a land unknown,
  A thirsty land, whose springs are dry.

2 Better than life itself Thy love,
  Dearer than all beside to me;
  For whom have I in Heaven above,
  Or what on Earth, compared with Thee?
          JAMES MONTGOMERY, 1822. *Abr.*

46   O Thou, Eternal, Changeless, Infinite!

10.10.10.10.10.   *"He is not far from each one of us."*   **Old 124th.**

M. W. S., 1882.

The Genevan Psalter.
LOUIS BOURGEOIS, 1551.

Largo.

1. O Thou, E - ter - nal, Changeless, In - fi - nite! First, Last and On - ly;

fill - ing all in all; Hid - ing Thy glo - ry in th' a - byss of light; Ma - jes - tic

in Thy mer - cy as Thy might; My God! with per - fect trust Thy name I call.

2 I dare, unfrightened, lift my eyes above;
   Within Thy house, my Father! can I fear?
   My heart's deep answer needeth not to prove
   The pulses of Thine omnipresent love;
   My spirit's cry Thy Spirit bends to hear.

3 Thou, Who the number of the stars dost tell,
   Bow, Lord, to order all my destiny!
   As seeing Thee who art invisible,
   Let me amid these awful grandeurs dwell,
   Forever Thine obedient child to be.

47 Praise, Lord, for Thee in Zion waits.

"*Assemble the people, the men and the women and the little ones, and thy stranger that is within thy gates that they may hear and that they may learn and fear the Lord.*"

L. M.   **Eisenach.**

HENRY F. LYTE, 1834. *Abr.*   JOHANN H. SCHEIN, 1628.

1. PRAISE, Lord, for Thee in Zi - on waits, Pray'r shall be - siege Thy tem - ple gates.

All flesh shall to Thy throne re - pair, And find, thro Christ, sal - va - tion there.

48

2 How blest Thy saints! how safely led!
How surely kept! how richly fed!
Saviour of all in earth and sea,
How happy they who rest in Thee!

3 Thy hand sets fast the mighty hills,
Thy voice the troubled ocean stills!
Evening and morning hymn Thy praise,
And Earth Thy bounty wide displays.

4 The year is with Thy goodness crowned;
Thy clouds drop wealth the world around;
Thro Thee the deserts laugh and sing,
And Nature smiles and owns her King.

5 Lord, on our souls Thy Spirit pour.
The moral waste within restore.
Oh let Thy love our spring-tide be,
And make us all bear fruit to Thee.

1 O SOURCE divine, and Life of all,
Thou Fount of being's wondrous sea,
Thy depth would every heart appall,
That saw not Love supreme in Thee.

2 We shrink before Thy vast abyss,
Where worlds on worlds eternal brood;
We know Thee truly but in this,
That Thou bestowest all our good.

3 And so, 'mid boundless time and space,
Oh grant us still in Thee to dwell,
And thro the ceaseless web to trace
Thy presence working all things well.

4 Bestow on every joyous thrill
Thy deeper tone of reverent awe;
Make pure Thy children's erring will,
And teach their hearts to love Thy law.

JOHN STERLING, 1839. *Abr.*

49 Lord of all being! throned afar.

L. M.   *"How precious are Thy thoughts unto me, O God."*   **Wareham.**

OLIVER WENDELL HOLMES, 1848.   WILLIAM KNAPP, 1738.

1. Lord of all be - ing! throned a - far, Thy glo - ry flames from Sun and star;

Cen - tre and soul of ev - ery sphere, Yet to each lov - ing heart how near.

50

2 Sun of our life, Thy quickening ray
Sheds on our path the glow of day;
Star of our hope, Thy softened light
Cheers the long watches of the night.

3 Our midnight is Thy smile withdrawn;
Our noontide is Thy gracious dawn;
Our rainbow arch Thy mercy's sign;
All, save the clouds of sin, are Thine.

4 Lord of all life, below, above,
Whose light is truth, whose warmth is love,
Before Thine ever-blazing throne
We ask no lustre of our own.

5 Grant us Thy truth to make us free,
And kindling hearts that burn for Thee,
Till all Thy living altars claim,
One holy light, one heavenly flame.

1 No human eyes Thy face may see,
No human thought Thy form may know:
But all creation dwells in Thee,
And Thy great life thro all doth flow!

2 And yet, oh strange and wondrous thought!
Thou art a God who hearest prayer,
And every heart with sorrow fraught
To seek Thy present aid may dare.

3 Yet Thou wilt turn them not aside
Who cannot solve Thy life divine,
But would give up all reason's pride
To know their hearts approved by Thine.

4 So tho we faint on life's dark hill,
And thought grow weak and knowledge
Yet faith shall teach us courage still, [flee,
And love shall guide us on to Thee.

THOMAS W. HIGGINSON, 1846.

51 Sing to the Lord a joyful song.

L. M. *"Let such as love Thy salvation say continually, the Lord be magnified."* **Intercession.**
JOHN S. B. MONSELL, 1862. ARR. JOHN B. DYKES, 1862.

1. Sing to the Lord a joy - ful song; Lift up your hearts, your voi - ces raise;

To us His gra - cious gifts be - long, To Him our songs of love and praise.

2 For life and love, for rest and food,
   For daily help and nightly care,
   Sing to the Lord, for He is good,
   And praise His Name, for it is fair.

3 For strength to those who on Him wait,
   His truth to prove, His will to do,
   Praise ye our God, for He is great,
   Trust in His Name, for it is true.

4 For joys untold that daily move
   Round those who love His sweet em-
   Sing to our God, for He is love, [ploy,
   Exalt His name, for it is joy.

5 For life below, with all its bliss,
   And for that life, more pure and high,
   That inner life, which over this
   Shall ever shine and never die.

52

1 My God, in whom are all the springs
   Of boundless love and grace unknown,
   Hide me beneath Thy spreading wings,
   Till the dark cloud is overblown.

2 Up to the heavens I send my cry;
   The Lord will my desires perform;
   He sends His angels from on high,
   And saves me from the threat'ning storm.

3 High o'er the Earth Thy mercy reigns,
   And reaches to the utmost sky;
   Thy truth to endless years remains,
   When lower worlds dissolve and die.

4 Be Thou exalted, O my God,
   Above the heavens where angels dwell;
   Thy power on Earth be known abroad,
   And land to land Thy wonders tell.

ISAAC WATTS, 1719. Abr.

53   My God, how wonderful Thou art!

C. M.   *" He healeth the broken in heart. He telleth the number of the stars."*   **Phuvah.**

FREDERICK W. FABER, 1849. *Abr.*   MELCHOIR VULPIUS, 1609.

1. My God, how won - der - ful Thou art! Thy maj - es - ty how bright!

How beau - ti - ful Thy mer - cy - seat, In depths of burn - ing light!

54

2 How dread are Thy eternal years,
O everlasting Lord!
By prostrate spirits, day and night,
Incessantly adored.

3 How beautiful, how beautiful,
The sight of Thee must be!—
Thine endless wisdom, boundless pow'r,
And awful purity!

4 Oh! how I fear Thee, living God!
With deepest, tenderest fears,
And worship Thee with trembling hope,
And penitential tears.

5 No earthly father loves like Thee,
No mother, half so mild,
Bears and forbears, as Thou hast done
With me, Thy sinful child.

1 I SING th' almighty power of God,
That made the mountains rise,
That spread the flowing seas abroad,
And built the lofty skies.

2 I sing the wisdom that ordained
The sun to rule the day;
The moon shines full at His command,
And all the stars obey.

3 Lord! how Thy wonders are displayed,
Where'er I turn mine eye,
If I survey the ground I tread,
Or gaze upon the sky!

4 There's not a plant or flower below,
But makes Thy glories known;
And clouds arise, and tempests blow,
By order from Thy throne.

ISAAC WATTS, 1715. *Abr.*

55 Oh, for a shout of joy!

6.6.6.6.8.8.

"In His temple everything saith—Glory!"

Sutherland.

J. Young, 1843. *Arr.*

William B. Bradbury, 1844.

1. { Oh, for a shout of joy! Wor - thy the theme we sing. }
{ To this di - vine em - ploy Our hearts and voic - es bring. } Sound, sound, thro

all...... the Earth.... a - broad,..The love,.... th'e - ter - nal love of God!

2 Thy Seraphs, bright and fair,
In countless myriads stand,
Veiling their faces there,
All bowed at Thy right hand:
Yet not their rapture's loudest chord
Can sound Thy wondrous love, O Lord!

3 Redeemed by sovereign grace,
Thy Church, in lower key,
Age-long, in every place,
Hath sung the mystery,—
Telling, in strains of sweet accord,
Thy love, Thy changeless love, O Lord!

56 Oh, bless the Lord, my soul!

S. M.

"Jehovah is my strength and my song."

State Street.

Thomas Cotterill, 1819.

Jonathan C. Woodman, 1844.

1. Oh, bless the Lord, my soul! His grace to thee pro-claim, And all that is with - in me join To bless His ho-ly name.

2 Oh! bless the Lord, my soul!
  His mercies bear in mind.
  Forget not all His benefits;
  The Lord to thee is kind.

3 He will not always chide;
  He will with patience wait;
  His wrath is ever slow to rise,
  And ready to abate.

4 He pardons all thy sins,
  Prolongs thy feeble breath,
  He healeth thine infirmities,
  And ransoms thee from death.

5 Then bless His holy name,
  Whose grace hath made thee whole!
  Whose loving-kindness crowns thy days;
  Oh! bless the Lord, my soul!

57 Praise to the Lord, the omnipotent King.

" Thou shalt be a pavilion for a shadow in the day-time from the heat, and for a refuge and for a covert from storm and from rain."

14.14.4.7.8.

Ger. JOACHIM NEANDER, 1679.
Tr. M. WOOLSEY STRYKER, 1882. *Abr.*

"Lobe den Herren."

JOACHIM NEANDER, 1665.

Animato.

1. { Praise to the Lord, the om - ni - po - tent King of Cre - a - - - tion! }
   { Join ye the cho - ral of Heav - en, O great congre - ga - - - tion! } My soul! par-take.

Ju - bi - lant psalm - o - dy wake, Pour forth thy glad in - vo - ca - - - tion!

2 Praise to the Lord! who in wonderful beauty hath made thee;
  Healed thee; and guided thee;—never neglected to aid thee!
    In bitter pain,
    Over and over again,
    God 'neath His covert hath stayed thee.

3 Praise to the Lord! He is reigning o'er all in His splendor,
  Yet, as on eagle-wing, beareth thee upward so tender!
    He hath decreed
    Bountifully to thy need;
    Deeply thy gratitude render.

58 How are Thy servants blest, O Lord!

C. M.   *"I know the thoughts that I think toward you."*   **Bemerton.**

JOSEPH ADDISON, 1772. *Abr.*   HENRY W. GREATOEX, 1849.

1. How are Thy serv - ants blest, O Lord! How sure is their de - fence!

E - ter - nal Wis - dom is their guide, Their help, Om - ni - po - tence.

2 In midst of dangers, fears, and deaths,
   Thy goodness we'll adore;
   We'll praise Thee for Thy mercies past,
   And humbly hope for more.

3 Our life, while Thou preserv'st that life,
   Thy sacrifice shall be;
   And death, when death shall be our lot,
   Shall join our souls to Thee.

59 Mighty God! while angels bless Thee.

" Lo, these are but the outskirts of His ways, and how small a whisper do we hear of Him."

8.7.8.7.   **Stockholm.**

ROBERT ROBINSON, 1774. *Abr.*   P. U. STENHAMMAR, d. 1884.

1. Might - y God! while an - gels bless Thee, May a mor - tal lisp Thy name? Lord of men, as

Praise to God.

Sounded thro the wide creation—
Be Thy just and awful praise.

3 For the grandeur of Thy nature,—
Grand, beyond a seraph's thought;
For the wonders of creation,—
Works with skill and kindness wrought;

4 For Thy providence, that governs
Thro Thine empire's wide domain,
Wings an angel, guides a sparrow;—
Blesséd be Thy gentle reign.

well as angels! Thou art every creature's theme.

2 Lord of every land and nation!
Ancient of eternal days!

60 God of my life! thro all my days.

L. M.   *" Thou hast known my soul in adversities."*   Grostete.

PHILIP DODDRIDGE, 1751.   HENRY W. GREATOREX, 1849.

1. God of my life! thro all my days,
My grate-ful pow'rs shall sound Thy praise;
The song shall wake with ope-ning light,
And war-ble to the si - lent night.

2 When anxious cares would break my rest,
And griefs would tear my throbbing breast,
Thy tuneful praises, raised on high,
Shall check the murmur and the sigh.

3 When death o'er nature shall prevail,
And all her powers of language fail;
Joy thro my swimming eyes shall break,
And mean the thanks I cannot speak.

4 But, oh! when that last conflict's o'er,
And I am chained to flesh no more,—
With what glad accents shall I rise
To join the music of the skies!

5 The cheerful tribute will I give,
Long as a deathless soul can live.
A work so sweet, a theme so high,
Demands and crowns eternity!

61   Our God, our help in ages past.

"Let the beauty of the Lord our God be upon us."

C. M. D.
ISAAC WATTS, 1719.

Norwich ("Old 137th.")
JOHN DAYE'S PSALTER, 1562.

1. Our God, our help in a - ges past, Our hope for years to come, Our shel - ter from the

storm - y blast, And our e - ter - nal home, Un - der the shad - ow of Thy throne, Thy

saints have dwelt se - cure; Suf - fi - cient is Thine arm a - lone, And our de - fense is sure.

2 Before the hills in order stood,
    Or Earth received her frame,
From everlasting Thou art God,
    To endless years the same.
A thousand ages, in Thy sight,
    Are like an evening gone,—
Short as the watch that ends the night,
    Before the rising Sun.

3 Time, like an ever-rolling stream,
    Bears all its sons away.
They fly, forgotten, as a dream
    Dies, at the opening day.
Our God, our help in ages past,
    Our hope for years to come,
Be Thou our Guard while troubles last,
    And our eternal Home!

Praise to God.

62   Lord! Thou hast been Thy people's rest.

"Thou art the same."

8.7.8.7.8.8.7.   **"Allein Gott in der Höh' sei Ehr."**

JAMES MONTGOMERY, 1821. *Abr.*   NICHOLAS DECIUS, 1539.
Har. FELIX MENDELSSOHN, 1835

Largo.

1. { LORD! Thou hast been Thy peo - ple's rest. Thro all their gen - e - ra - tions. }
{ Their ref - uge when by dan - gers prest, Their hope in trib - u - la - tions; }

Thou, ere the mountains sprang to birth, Or ev - er Thou hadst formed the Earth,

Art God from ev - er - last - ing!

2 Lord! teach us so to mark our days
  That we may prize them duly;
So guide our feet in wisdom's ways
  That we may love Thee truly;
Return, O Lord, our griefs behold,
And with Thy goodness, as of old,
  Oh satisfy us early!

63

1 To GOD on high be thanks and praise,
  For mercies none can sever,
Whereby no foe a hand can raise,
  And harm can reach us never.

To Him with joy our hearts ascend,
The source of peace that knows no end,
  Forever and forever!

From NICHOLAS DECIUS, 1529.

64 The God of Abraham praise.

0.6.8.4, D.   *"If ye are Christ's, then are ye Abraham's seed."*   **Uriel.**

THOMAS OLIVERS, 1772. *Abr.*   M. WOOLSEY STRYKER, 1883.

1. The God of A - bra'm praise, Who reigns en - throned a - bove, The An - cient of e - ter - nal days, And God of Love! JE - HO-VAH,—great I AM! By Earth and Heav'n con - fest; I bow, and bless the sa - cred Name, For ev - er blest!

Copyright, 1883, by Biglow & Main.

2 The God of Abra'm praise!
    At whose supreme command
From Earth I rise, and seek the joys
    At His right hand.
I all on Earth forsake,
    Its wisdom, fame, and power;
And Him my only portion make,
    My Shield and Tower.

3 He by Himself hath sworn;
    I on His oath depend;
I shall, on eagles' wings upborne,
    To Heaven ascend.
I shall behold His face,
    I shall His power adore,
And sing the wonders of His grace
    Forevermore!

65   When all Thy mercies, O my God.

C. M.   *"When I said 'My foot slippeth!' Thy mercy. O Lord, held me up."*   **Geneva.**

JOSEPH ADDISON, 1728. *Abr.*   JOHN COLE, 1800.

1. WHEN all   Thy mer - cies, O   my   God! My ris - ing soul sur - veys,
When all   Thy mer - cies, O   my   God!

When all Thy mercies, O my God!

f

Trans-port - ed with   the view I'm   lost, In   won - der, love, and praise.

Trans - ported with the view   I'm   lost,

2 Ten thousand thousand precious gifts
   My daily thanks employ;
Nor is the least a cheerful heart,
   That tastes those gifts with joy.

3 Thro all eternity, to Thee
   A joyful song I'll raise:
For, oh! eternity's too short
   To utter all Thy praise.

66   Glory be to the Father.

Single Chant.   *"He hath set eternity in their heart."*   **The Gloria Patri.**

1. GLORY be to the Father, and.......... | to the | Son, | And.......... | to the | Ho - ly | Ghost!
2. As it was in the beginning, is now, and | ev - er | shall be, | World........ | without | end, A- | men.

67 The Lord is King! Lift up Thy voice.

L. M.
JOSIAH CONDER, 1824. Abr.

"Who hath blessed us with every spiritual blessing."

Octavius.
L. VAN BEETHOVEN, 1813.
Arr. GEO. F. ROOT, 1849.

1. The Lord is King! Lift up thy voice, O Earth, and all ye Heav'ns, re-joice;
From world to world the joy shall ring, The Lord Om-ni-po-tent is King!

2 Alike pervaded by His eye,
All parts of His dominion lie;
This world of ours and worlds unseen,—
There is no boundary between.

3 Oh, when His wisdom can mistake,
His might decay, His love forsake,
Then may His children cease to sing,
The Lord Omnipotent is King.

68 O Holy, Heavenly Lord.

6s & 4s.
M. W. S., 1890.

"Which was, and Which is, and Which is to come."

Italian Hymn.
FELIX GIARDINI, 1769. Alt.

1. O Ho-ly, Heav'n-ly Lord, By worlds on worlds a-dored, To whom al-way Fire-wing-èd

Praise to God.

cher - u - bim And ra-diant ser - a-phim Lift their un - ceas-ing hymn, And homage pay!

2 We too, Thou only King,
That chorus answering,
    Would swell the strain,
Trumpet and cymbal tone
Sound to Thy burning throne
With all the ransomed, own
    Thy blessèd reign.

3 Oh, what a gathering
When God's whole Church shall sing!
    What raptures then!
For that bright symphony
Of immortality
May we all numbered be,
    Thro Christ! Amen.

69   God be merciful unto us, and bless us.

Double Chant.   *"There was great joy in that city."*   **Bonn.**

PSALM LXVII.   LUDWIG VAN BEETHOVEN.

1. GOD be merciful, etc.   2. That Thy way, etc.

1 GOD be merciful unto | us, and | bless us, || And cause His | face to | shine up- | on us. ||
2 That Thy way may be | known upon | Earth, || Thy saving | health a- | mong all | nations. ||

3 Let the peoples praise | Thee, O | God; || Let | all the | peoples | praise Thee. ||
4 Oh let the nations be glad and | sing for | joy; || For Thou shalt judge the peoples
    with equity, and lead the | nations | upon | Earth. ||

5 Let the peoples praise | Thee, O | God; || Let | all the | peoples | praise Thee. ||
6 The Earth hath yielded her increase: God, even our own | God, shall | bless us. ||
    God shall bless us, And all the ends of the | Earth shall | fear | Him. ||

70   Therefore with angels and archangels.

Chant.   "*They shall abundantly utter the memory of Thy great goodness.*"   **The Trisagion.**

The Third Century, A. D.   John Camidge.

Therefore with angels and archangels, } { laud and
and with all the company of .... } Heav'n, we { magnify Thy } glorious Name; { evermore } prising

Thee, and | say-ing;—| Ho - ly, | Ho - ly, | Ho - ly, | Lord God of | Hosts! | Heav'n and | Earth

are | full of Thy | glo-ry. | Glo - ry | be..... to | Thee, O | Lord Most | High! | A - men.

71   Joy to the world! The Lord is come!

C. M.   "*This is the Heir.*"   **Christmas.**

Isaac Watts, 1709. *Abr.*   George F. Handel, 1728.

1. Joy   to the world! The Lord is   come! Let Earth receive her   King!   Let   ev - 'ry

The Nativity.

heart pre - pare Him room, And Heav'n and Na - ture sing, And Heav'n and Na - ture sing.

2 Joy to the Earth! The Saviour reigns!
  Let men their songs employ;
  While fields and floods, rocks, hills and
  Repeat the sounding joy.   [plains

3 He rules the world with truth and grace,
  And makes the nations prove
  The glories of His righteousness,
  And wonders of His love.

72   All the hosts of morning sing.

7.8.7.8.7.7.   "A little child shall lead them."   Zuversicht.
M. W. S. 1885.   JOHANN CRÜGER, 1653.

1. { ALL the hosts of morning sing, All the chimes of Heav'n are swing - ing }
   { All the air is qua-ver - ing, All the star - ry depths are ring - ing } O'er the shepherds

with their flocks, God's e- ter - nal world un - locks.

3 Birth-night of the Son of Man,
    Virgin's Child, yet Lord Almighty!
  Still toward Bethlehem's crowded khan
    Sings the world its glad *Venite!*
  Star-led where the Christ-babe lies,
  Throng with gifts the heavenly wise.

2 Swiftly down the lustrous skies
    Angels troop with salutation,—
  'Mid unearthly minstrelsies,
    Tell the Saviour's incarnation.
  "Fear no longer, HE is come,
  Judah's heir, in David's home!"

4 Who His humble vigils keep
    Christ doth bless with new evangels.
  They who feed the Saviour's sheep
    Oft shall hear the song of angels.
  God's high glory yet fulfills
  Peace, to men of gentle wills.

73 There burns a star o'er Bethlehem town.

8.8.8.8.8.8.
EUGENE FIELD, 1889.

"Where is the way to the dwelling of Light!"

Peniel.
JOSIAH BOOTH, 1888.

1. THERE burns a star o'er Bethlehem town, And glo - rious - ly it beam - eth down

Up - on a vir - gin moth - er meek, And Him whom sol - emn Ma - gi seek.

Burn on, O star! and be the light To guide us all to Him this night!

2 The angels walk in Bethlehem town,—
The angels come and bring a crown
To Him, our Saviour and our King,
And sweetly all this night they sing.
Sing on in rapture, angel throng!
That we may learn that heavenly song!

3 Near Bethlehem town there blooms a
And it shall stand on Calvary!   [tree,
But from the shade thereof we turn

Unto the star that still shall burn,
When Christ is dead and risen again,
To mind us that He died for men.

4 There is a cry in Bethlehem town!
'Tis of the Babe that wears the crown.
It telleth us that man is free,—
That He redeemeth all and me!
The night is sped—behold the morn!
Sing, O my soul, the Christ is born!

The Nativity.

74 Brightest and best of the sons of the morning.

11.10.11.10. *" Mine eyes have seen Thy salvation."* **St. Laura.**

REGINALD HEBER, 1811. WILLIAM ALEX. BARRETT, 1850.

1. BRIGHTEST and best of the sons of the morn-ing! Dawn on our darkness, and lend us Thine aid.

Star of the East, the ho - ri - zon a - dorn - ing, Guide where our in - fant Redeem-er is laid.

2 Cold on His cradle the dew-drops are shining,
 Low lies His head with the beasts of the stall:
Angels adore Him, in slumber reclining,
 Maker, and Monarch, and Saviour of all.

3 Say, shall we yield Him, in costly devotion,
 Odors of Edom, and offerings divine,
Gems from the mountain, and pearls from the ocean,
 Myrrh from the forest, or gold from the mine?

4 Vainly we offer each ample oblation,
 Vainly with gold would His favor secure:
Richer, by far, is the heart's adoration,
 Dearer to God are the prayers of the poor.

5 Brightest and best are the sons of the morning!
 Dawn on our darkness, and lend us Thine aid.
Star of the East, the horizon adorning,
 Guide where our infant Redeemer is laid.

75

O little town of Bethlehem.

C. M. D.   *"They are dead which sought the young Child's life."*   **St. Silvester.**

PHILLIPS BROOKS, 1865.   JOSEPH BARNBY, 1867.

1. O LIT- TLE town of Beth - le- hem! How still we see thee lie, A- bove thy deep and dream-less

sleep,The si- lent stars go by: Yet in thy dark streets shineth The ev - er-last-ing Light; The hopes and

cres.

rit.

fears of all the years, Are met in thee to - night.

2 For Christ is born of Mary,
   And gathered all above,
While mortals sleep, the angels keep
   Their watch of wondering love.
O morning stars, together
   Proclaim the holy birth!
And praises sing to God the King,
   And peace to men on Earth!

3 How silently, how silently,
   The wondrous gift is given!
So God imparts to human hearts
   The blessings of His Heaven.
No ear may hear His coming,
   But in this world of sin,
Where meek souls will receive Him, still
   The dear Christ enters in.

4 O holy Child of Bethlehem,
   Descend to us, we pray,
Cast out our sin, and enter in,
   Be born in us to-day!
We hear the Christmas angels
   The great glad tidings tell;
O come to us, abide with us,
   Our Lord Emmanuel!

76 O come, all ye faithful.

P. M. *"To guide our feet into the way of peace."* **Adeste Fideles.**

Latin, 15th or 16th Century.
Tr. FREDERICK OAKELEY, 1841. Abr. & Alt.

MARC ANTOINE PORTOGALLO, 1790.

1. O come, all ye faith-ful, joy-ful-ly tri-umph-ant, To Beth-le-hem hast-en now with glad ac-cord; Lo! in a man-ger Lies the King of an-gels; O come, let us a-dore Him, O come, let us a-dore Him. O come, let us a-dore Him, Christ the Lord.

2 Sing forth, choirs of angels, sing in exultation,
  Thro Heaven's highest arches be your praises poured!
  Now to our God be glory in the highest!—
  O come, let us adore Him, Christ the Lord!

3 Amen! Lord we bless Thee, born for our salvation,—
  O Jesus, forever be Thy Name adored!
  Word of the Father, now for man Incarnate;—
  O come, let us adore Him, Christ the Lord!

The Nativity.

77 It came upon the midnight clear.

C. M. D. *"When the kindness of God our Saviour, and His love toward man appeared."* **Carol.**

EDMUND H. SEARS, 1849. *Abr.* RICHARD STORRS WILLIS, 1849.

1. It came up - on the midnight clear—That glorious song of old, From an - gels bend-ing

near the Earth To touch their harps of gold: "Peace on the Earth, good-will to men From

Heav'ns all-gracious King!"— The world in sol - emn still - ness lay To hear the An - gels sing.

2 Still thro the cloven skies they came,
  With peaceful wings unfurled;
And still their heavenly music floats
  O'er all the weary world;
Above its sad and lowly plains
  They bend on hov'ring wing,
And ever o'er its Babel-sounds,
  The blessèd angels sing.

3 Yet, with the woes of sin and strife
  The world has suffered long;
Beneath the angel-strain have rolled
  Two thousand years of wrong;
And man, at war with man, hears not
  The love-song which they bring:
Oh! hush the noise, ye men of strife,
  And hear the angels sing!

78 Calm on the listening ear of night.

C. M.   *"The Desire of all nations."*   **Lanarkshire.**

EDMUND H. SEARS, 1834. *Abr.*   MITCHISON'S HARMONY, Glasgow, 1849.

1. Calm on the list-'ning ear of night Come Heav'n's me - lo - dious strains, Where wild Ju - de - a stretch - es far Her sil - ver - man - tled plains.

2 Celestial choirs, from courts above,
Shed sacred glories there,
And angels, with their sparkling lyres,
Make music on the air.

3 The answering hills of Palestine
Send back the glad reply,
And greet, from all their holy heights,
The day-spring from on high.

4 O'er the blue depths of Galilee
There comes a holier calm,
And Sharon waves, in solemn praise,
Her silent groves of palm.

5 Light on thy hills, Jerusalem!
The Saviour now is born;
And bright,on Bethlehem's joyous plains,
Breaks the first Christmas morn.

79

1 COME, Thou, with purifying fire,
And swift-dividing sword,
Thou of all nations the Desire,
Earth waits Thy cleansing word.

2 Struck by the lightning of Thy glance,
Let old oppressions die;
Before Thy cloudless countenance
Let fear and falsehood fly.

3 Anoint our eyes with healing grace,
To see, as not before,
Our Father in our brother's face,
Our Maker in His poor.

4 How late Thy bright and awful brow
Breaks thro these clouds of sin;
Hail, Truth divine! we know Thee *now*,
Angel of God, come in!

ELIZA SCUDDER, 1860. *Abr.*

80   What grace, O Lord! and beauty shone.

C. M.   " *Whosoever shall do the will of God, the same is My brother.*"   **Horsley.**

EDWARD DENNY, 1839.   WILLIAM HORSLEY, 1815.

1. WHAT grace, O Lord! and beau-ty shone A-round Thy steps be-low! What pa-tient love was seen in all Thy life and death of woe!

2 Forever on Thy burdened heart
A weight of sorrow hung;
Yet no ungentle, murmuring word
Escaped Thy silent tongue.

3 Thy foes might hate, despise, revile,
Thy friends unfaithful prove;
Unwearied in forgiveness still,
Thy heart could only love.

4 Oh give us hearts to love like Thee,
Like Thee, O Lord, to grieve
Far more for others' sins, than all
The wrongs that we receive.

5 One with Thyself, may every eye
In us, Thy brethren, see
The gentleness and grace that springs
From union, Lord, with Thee.

81   Fierce raged the tempest.

8.8.8.3.   " *Why are ye fearful? Have ye not yet faith?*"   **St. Aelred.**

GODFREY THRING, 1858.   JOHN B. DYKES, 1862.

1. FIERCE raged the tempest o'er the deep, Watch did Thine anxious servants keep. But Thou wast wrapt in

Christ's Ministry.

guile-less sleep, Calm and still. A - men.

2 "Save, Lord, we perish," was their cry,
"O save us in our agony!"

Thy word above the storm rose high.
"Peace, be still."

3 The wild winds hushed; the angry deep
Sank, like a little child, to sleep;
The sullen billows cease to leap,
At Thy will.

4 So, when our life is clouded o'er,
And storm-winds drift us from the shore,
Say, lest we sink to rise no more,
"Peace, be still." *Amen.*

82   Fierce was the Galilee.

6s & 4s, D.   *"Who then is this, that even the wind and the sea obey Him?"*   **Faith.**

Gk. ANATOLIUS, 458.
Tr. JOHN M. NEALE, 1862. *Alt.*   JAMES FLINT, 1873.

1. FIERCE was the Gal - i - lee. Dark was the night. Oars labored heav - i - ly. Foam glimmer'd white.

Trembled the mar - i - ners. Per - il was high. Then said the God of God, "Peace! it is I!"

2 Ridge of the mountain-wave,
   Lower thy crest!
Wail of Euraquilo,
   Be thou at rest!
Sorrow can never be,
   Darkness must fly,
Where saith the Light of light,
m.   "Peace! it is I!"

3 Jesus, Deliverer,
   Come Thou to me.
Soothe Thou my voyaging
   Over life's sea.
Thou, when the storm of death
   Roars, sweeping by,
Whisper, Thou Truth of truth,
p.   "Peace! it is I!"

83 My dear Redeemer, and my Lord!

L. M.   *"All wondered at the words of grace which proceeded out of His mouth."*   **Germany.**

ISAAC WATTS, 1709.   LUDWIG VAN BEETHOVEN, 1825. *Arr.*

1. My dear Re - deem-er, and my Lord! I read my du - ty in Thy word:

But, in Thy life, the law ap - pears Drawn out in liv - ing char - ac - ters!

2 Such was Thy truth, and such Thy zeal,
Such deference to Thy Father's will,
Such love, and meekness so divine,
I would transcribe and make them mine.

3 Cold mountains and the midnight air
Witnessed the fervor of Thy prayer;

The desert Thy temptations knew,
Thy conflict and Thy victory, too.

4 Be Thou my pattern. Make me bear
More of Thy gracious image here;
Then God, the Judge, shall own my name
Among the followers of the Lamb.

84 Ride on! Ride on in majesty!

L. M.   *"THIS IS JESUS THE KING."*   **Drostane.**

HENRY HART MILMAN, 1821. *Abr.*   JOHN B. DYKES, 1859.

1. Ride on! Ride on in maj - es - ty! Hark! all the tribes Ho-san - na cry. O Saviour meek, pursue Thy road

Christ's Ministry.

With palms and scat-ter'd garments strew'd.

2 Ride on, ride on in majesty!
The wingèd squadrons of the sky
Look down with sad and wondering eyes
To see th'approaching sacrifice.

3 Ride on, ride on in majesty!
In lowly pomp, ride on to die.
Bow Thy meek head to mortal pain,
Then take, O God, Thy power, and reign.

85   Hosanna to the Living Lord!

8.8.8.8.11.   "*If these shall hold their peace, the stones will cry out.*"   **Hosanna.**
REGINALD HEBER, 1811.   JOHN B. DYKES, 1876.

1. Ho - san-na to the liv-ing Lord! Ho - san-na to th'In-carnate Word To Christ, Cre - a-tor,

After each Stanza.

Saviour, King, Let Earth, let Heav'n, Hosanna sing! Ho - san-na, LORD! Ho-san-na IN THE HIGH - EST!

2 Hosanna, Lord, Thine angels cry.
Hosanna, Lord, Thy saints reply.
Above, beneath us, and around,
The dead and living swell the sound.

3 O Saviour, with protecting care,
Return to this Thy house of prayer,
Assembled in Thy sacred name.
Here we Thy parting promise claim.

4 But chiefest in our cleansèd breast,
Eternal, bid Thy Spirit rest,
And make our secret soul to be
A temple pure, and worthy Thee!

5 So, in the last and dreadful day,
When Earth and Heaven shall melt away,
Thy flock, redeemed from sinful stain,
Shall swell the sound of praise again.

86 Now they all have denied Him.

7.6.7.7.9.3. "*Behoved it not the Christ to suffer these things?*" **Stabat Mater.**
M. W. S., 1689. *Abr.* CHARLES FRANÇOIS GOUNOD, 1881, *Arr.* B. C. B., 1890.

1. Now they all have de-nied Him! Straight to the death guide Him; So have they cru-ci - fied Him,
2. 'Mid the tu-mult and rail - ing, Hark! his last breath fail - ing, Prayeth the thief pre-vail - ing,

Mal - o - fac-tors be - side Him.— "Fa - ther, pit - y them; they do not know What they do!"
"Lord, re-member me!" wail - ing. — "Ay, in Par - a - dise soon shalt thou be Safe with Me!"

Copyright, 1891, by The Biglow & Main Co.

3 Deeper darkness is falling,
  Even the Christ thralling.
  Listen! that cry appalling,
  From what depths it is calling:
"*Ah, My God, why forsakest Thou Me?*
  Eloi!"

4 Bowed His head to sin's wages,
  Hatred in vain rages,
  Cleft is the Rock of Ages,
  Answered prophecy's pages.
"*Finished!*" Finished! The agony done!
  Life is won!

87 O Jesus, sweet the tears I shed.

C. M. "*Our great God and Saviour, Jesus Christ.*" **Medfield.**
RAY PALMER, 1867. *Abr.* WILLIAM MATHER, 1790.
Har. RICHARD S. WILLIS, 1849.

1. O Je - sus, sweet the tears I shed, While at Thy cross I kneel,
2. 'Twas for the sin - ful Thou didst die, And I a sin - ner stand;

The Cross.

Gaze on Thy wounded, faint - ing head, And all Thy sor - rows feel!
What love speaks from Thy dy - ing eye, And from each pierc - ed hand!

3 I know this cleansing blood of Thine
  Was shed, dear Lord, for me,—
For me, for all, O grace divine!
  Who look by faith on Thee.

4 In patient hope, my cross I'll bear,
  Thine arm shall be my stay;
And Thou, enthroned, my soul shalt spare,
  On Thy great judgment-day.

88   O Lamb of God, unspotted.

" Him who knew no sin, He made to be sin on our behalf; that we might become
the righteousness of God in Him."

7s & 9, P.
Ger. NICOLAUS DECIUS, 1523. Tr. M. W. S., 1884.

Agnus Dei.
NICOLAUS DECIUS, 1541.

1. { O Lamb of God un - spot - ted, Whose life that cross hath tak - en, }
   { All calm in grief al - lot - ted, How - e'er Thou wert for - sak - en, } All sin Thou hast en-

dur - ed, Else were no hope as - sur - ed; Have mer-cy up - on us, O Je - sus!

2 Thy name the full heart blesses,
  That Thou relief so thoro
Hast wrought for our distresses.
  Give us a godly sorrow,
That we our sins may vanquish,
  Remembering Thine anguish;
Have mercy upon us, O Jesus.

3 Our confidence embolden
  Thro Thy vicarious grieving,
That, steadfastly upholden,
  And ne'er Thy presence leaving,
We die at last unshaken,
  And safe in Heaven awaken;
Grant unto us Thy peace, O Jesus!

89   When I survey the wondrous Cross.

" That a death having taken place for the redemption of the transgressions that were under the first covenant, they
that have been called may receive the promise of the eternal inheritance."

L. M.

ISAAC WATTS, 1709. *Arr.*

Hamburg.

First Gregorian Tone, A. D. 590.
Arr. LOWELL MASON, 1824.

1. WHEN I sur-vey the won-drous Cross On which the Prince of Glo-ry died,
My rich-est gain I count but loss, And pour con-tempt on all my pride.

90

2 Forbid it, Lord, that I should boast,
Save in the death of Christ, my God;
All the vain things that charm me most,
I sacrifice them to His blood.

3 See, from His head, His hands, His feet,
Sorrow and love flow mingled down!
Did e'er such love and sorrow meet,
Or thorns compose so rich a crown?

4 Oh, the sweet wonders of that Cross,
Where God the Saviour loved and died!
Her noblest life my spirit draws   [side.
From His dear wounds and bleeding

5 Were the whole realm of nature mine,
That were a present far too small;
Love so amazing, so divine,
Demands my soul, my life, my all!

1 LORD JESUS, when we stand afar,
And gaze upon Thy holy Cross,
In love of Thee and scorn of self,
Oh, may we count the world as loss!

2 When we behold Thy bleeding wounds,
And the rough way that Thou hast trod,
Make us to hate the load of sin
That lay so heavy on our God.

3 O holy Lord! uplifted high,
With outstretch'd arms, in mortal woe,
Embracing in Thy wondrous love
The sinful world that lies below!

4 Give us an ever-living faith
To gaze beyond the things we see,
And in the mystery of Thy death
Draw us and all men after Thee!

WILLIAM W. HOW, 1854.

91   Lo! where that spotless Lamb.

"Behoved it not the Christ to suffer these things, and to enter into His glory!"

11.11.11.5.   **"Herzliebster Jesu."**

M. W. S., 1884.   JOHANN CRUGER, 1640.

1 Lo! where that spot-less Lamb, for sin pro - vid - ed, Thorned, bruised a-bandoned, tor-tured and de - rid - ed, Pours out His soul for human ransom, yon-der, While an-gels won - der!

2 Jesus, what woe Thy love for us hath won Thee!
  For God hath laid our chastisement upon Thee,
    From our deep guilt Thy death its anguish borrows—
      Thou Man of Sorrows!

3 Crucified Saviour, by Thy mortal passion,
  By the dark travail that hath wrought salvation,
    Hear, Lord, a sinner, all his shame deploring,
      Thy grace adoring!

4 Christ, I have wronged Thee! penitent, heart-broken,
  Justly condemned;—yet be Thy mercy spoken!
    O Prince of Life, let this Thy strange enthronement
      Be mine atonement!

5 Glories undimmed are Thine, Thou King of Ages,
  Whose name Thy Church in thankful hymns engages.
    To God, thro Thee, in constant sacrifices,
      Her praise uprises!

92 O sacred Head, now wounded.

"This is My blood of the covenant which is shed for many unto remission of sins."

7s & 6s, D.

Ger. (a trans. from the Latin) PAUL GERHARDT, 1656.
Tr. JAMES W. ALEXANDER, 1829, Abr.

Passion Chorale.

JOHANN LEONARD HASLER, 1601.
Har. JOHANN SEBASTIAN BACH, 1729.

1. { O Sa - cred Head, now wound-ed, With grief and shame weighed down, }
   { Now scorn-ful - ly sur - round-ed With thorns,—Thine on - ly crown, }

O Sa - cred Head, what glo - ry, What bliss, till now was Thine!

Yet, tho de - spised and go - - ry, I joy to call Thee mine.

2 What Thou, my Lord! hast suffered
  Was all for sinners' gain;
  Mine, mine was the transgression,
  But Thine the deadly pain.
  Lo! here I fall, my Saviour!
  'Tis I deserve Thy place.
  Look on me with Thy favor,
  Vouchsafe to me Thy grace.

3 What language shall I borrow
  To thank Thee, dearest Friend!
  For this Thy dying sorrow,
  Thy pity without end!
  Oh! make me Thine for ever;
  And, should I fainting be,
  Lord! let me never, never,
  Outlive my love to Thee!

93 Blessèd word, my soul awaking.

"As many as shall walk by this rule, peace be upon them, and mercy, and upon the Israel of God."

8s. 7s. & 3s. P.
M. W. S., 1890.

Paradox.
Benjamin C. Blodgett, 1890.

1. Bless-ed word, my soul a - wak - ing, Je - sus died! Eyes that weep and hearts a-breaking,

Je - sus died! Mu-sic ne'er with quiv-'ring string, Can such sounds of rap - ture bring, As when

His dear name we sing. Je - sus died!

2 Fear we naught of wrath infernal,
  Jesus died!
He hath power of life eternal,
  Jesus died!
Son of God and Son of Man,
Light of Life ere time began,
Mercy is Thy mighty plan!
  Jesus died!

3 Christ is still with them that love Him,—
  Jesus died!
Still doth work with them that prove
  Jesus died! [Him,—
Still He heareth them that pray,
Still He taketh sins away,
Turneth night to beauteous day,
  Jesus died!

4 When at last the veil is rending,—
  Jesus died!
Stars are falling, skies are bending;
  Jesus died!
Then with boldness this shall be
All my trust and all my plea,—
Lord, that day remember me!—
  Jesus died!

94 Thou, O Most Compassionate!

7.7.7.7.
JOHN G. WHITTIER, 1855. *Abr.*

"*Make it as sure as ye can.*"

Solitude.
LEWIS T. DOWNES, 1850.

1. Thou, O Most Com - pas - sion - ate! Who didst stoop to our es - tate,

Drink - ing of the cup we drain, Tread - ing in our path of pain.—

2 Thro the doubt and mystery,
Grant to us Thy steps to see,
And the grace to draw from thence
Larger hope and confidence.

3 Show Thy vacant tomb, and let,
As of old, the angels yet
Whisper by its open door,—
"Fear not! He hath gone before!"

95 O sons and daughters, let us sing!

8.8.8.4.
Lat Twelfth Century.
Tr. JOHN M. NEALE, 1861. *Abr.*

"*Open Thou mine eyes.*"

Victory.
GIOVANNI PALESTRINA, 1545.

1. O sons and daughters, let us sing! The King of Heav'n, the glo - rious King, O'er death to -

The Resurrection.

day rose tri-umph-ing.   AL-LE-LU - IA!

2 When Thomas first the tidings heard,
He doubted if it were his Lord,
Until He came and spake that word.

3 How blest are they who do not see!
And yet whose faith is firm in Thee;
For they shall live eternally.

4 On this most holy day of days,
To Thee our heart and voice we raise
In laud, and jubilee, and praise.

96   We saw Thee not when Thou didst come.

8.8.8.8.8.8.   " Blessed are they that have not seen and yet have believed."   Wavertree.

JOHN HAMPDEN GURNEY, 1838, 1851.   WILLIAM SHORE, 1840. Alt.

1. WE saw Thee not when Thou didst come To this poor world of sin and death,
Nor e'er be - held Thy cot- tage home In that de - spis - ed Naz - a - reth: But we be- lieve Thy

foot-steps trod Its streets and plains, Thou Son of God!

2 We did not see Thee lifted high,
Amid that wild and ribald crew;
Nor heard Thy meek imploring cry—
"*Forgive, they know not what they do!*"
Yet we believe the deed was done
Which shook the Earth and veiled the Sun.

3 We stood not by the empty tomb
Where late Thy sacred body lay,

Nor sat within that upper room,
Nor met Thee in the open way:
But we believe that angels said,
'Why seek the living 'mong the dead?'

4 We did not mark the chosen few,
When Thou didst thro the clouds ascend,
First lift to Heaven their wondering view,
Then to the earth all prostrate bend:
Yet we believe that mortal eyes
Beheld that journey to the skies.

5 And now that Thou dost reign on high,
And thence Thy waiting people bless,
No ray of glory from the sky
Doth shine upon our wilderness:
But we believe Thy faithful word,
And trust in our redeeming Lord.

The Resurrection.

97   Come, ye faithful, raise the strain.

7s & 6s, D.   *"In Him is the Yea; wherefore also thro Him is the Amen."*   **St. Kevin.**

Gk. John of Damascus, cir. 780.
Tr, John M. Neale, 1862, Abr.   Arthur S. Sullivan, 1872.

1. COME, ye faith-ful, raise the strain Of tri-umph-ant glad-ness! God hath brought His Is-ra-el In-to joy from sad-ness.— Loosed from Pharaoh's bit-ter yoke Ja-cob's sons and daughters,— Led them, with unmoistened feet, Thro the Red Sea wa-ters.

2 'Tis the spring of souls to-day;
  Christ hath burst His prison,
And from three days sleep in death
  As the Sun hath risen.
All the winter of our sins,
  Long and dark, is flying
From His light, to whom we give
  Laud and praise undying.

3 Neither might the gates of death,
  Nor the tomb's dark portal,
Nor the watchers, nor the seal,
  Hold Thee as a mortal:
But to-day amidst the Twelve
  Thou didst stand, bestowing
Thine own peace, which evermore
  Passeth human knowing.

98   Christ, the Lord, is risen to-day.

7s & 4s, P.   *"Thou didst cleave the fountain and the flood."*   **Easter Hymn.**

CHARLES WESLEY, 1739.   LYRA DAVIDICA, 1708.

Animato.

1. CHRIST, the Lord, is risen to-day, AL - - - - LE - LU - IA! Sons of men, and an - gels, say; AL - - - - LE - LU - IA! Raise your joys and tri-umphs high! AL - - - - LE - LU - IA! Sing, ye Heav'ns! and Earth, re-ply! AL - - - - LE - LU - IA!

2 Love's redeeming work is done,
  Fought the fight, the battle won;
  Lo, our Sun's eclipse is o'er;
  Lo, He sets in blood no more.

3 Vain the stone, the watch, the seal;
  Christ hath burst the gates of hell;
  Death in vain forbids His rise;
  Christ hath opened Paradise.

4 Lives again our glorious King;
  "Where, O Death, is now thy sting?"
  Once He died our souls to save;
  "Where's thy victory, boasting Grave?"

5 Soar we now where Christ has led,
  Following our exalted Head;
  Made like Him, like Him we rise;
  Ours the cross, the grave, the skies!

99
Thou art gone up on high.

S. M.   *"While He blest them, He parted from them."*   **St. Philip.**

EMMA L. TOKE, 1851.   EDWARD J. HOPKINS, 1850.

1 THOU art gone up on high
  To mansions in the skies,
And round Thy throne unceasingly
  Glad songs of praise arise.

2 But we are lingering here
  With sin and care opprest;
Lord, send Thy promised Comforter,
  And lead us to Thy rest.

3 Thou art gone up on high:
  But Thou didst first come down,
Thro Earth's most bitter agony,
  To pass unto Thy crown;

4 And girt with griefs and fears
  Our onward course must be:
But only let that path of tears
  Lead us at last to Thee.

5 Thou art gone up on high:
  But Thou shalt come again,
With all the bright ones of the sky
  Attendant in Thy train.

6 Oh, by Thy saving power,
  So make us live and die,
That we may stand in that dread hour,
  At Thy right hand on high.

100
The golden gates lift up their heads.

C. M.   *"If it be of God ye cannot overthrow it."*   **Belgrave.**

CECIL F. ALEXANDER, 1858.   WILLIAM HORSLEY, 1828.

1. The gold - en gates lift up their heads, The doors are o - pened wide.

The Ascension.

The King of glo - ry is gone up Un - to His Fa - ther's side.

2 Thou art gone in before us, Lord,
  Thou hast prepared a place,
  That we may be where now Thou art,
  And look upon Thy face.

3 And ever on Thine earthly path
  A gleam of glory lies,
  A light still breaks behind the cloud
  That veils Thee from our eyes.

4 Lift up our thoughts, lift up our songs,
  And let Thy grace be given,
  That while we linger yet below
  Our hearts may be in Heaven,—

5 That where Thou art at God's right hand
  Our hope, our love may be;
  Dwell in us now, that we may dwell
  For evermore in Thee.

101   He is gone! and we remain.

7.7.7.7.   " It is expedient for you that I go away."   Nuremburg.
ARTHUR PENRHYN STANLEY, 1862. Abr.   JOHANN RUDOLPH AHLE, 1664.

1. { He is gone! and we re-main In this world of sin and pain, }
   { In the void which He has left. On this Earth of Him be - reft: }
   We have still His

work to do, We can still His path pursue.

Forward all our glances cast;
Still His words before us range
Thro the ages, as they change.

3 He is gone! but we once more
  Shall behold Him as before,
  In the Heaven of heavens the same
  As on Earth He went and came.
  In that world, unseen, unknown,
  He and we shall yet be one!

2 He is gone! unto their goal
  World and Church must onward roll;
  Far behind we leave the past;

The Holy Ghost.

102

O Word of God Incarnate.

7s & 6s, D.

"The testimony of Jesus, is the spirit of prophecy."

Munich.

William W. How, 1857.

Johann Herman, 1620.
Har. Felix Mendelssohn, 1847.

1. O Word of God In - car - nate, O Wis - dom from on high, O Truth unchanged, un - chang - ing, O Light of our dark sky; We praise Thee for the ra - diance That from the hal - lowed page, A lan - tern to our foot-steps, Shines on from age to age.

2 The Church from Thee, her Master,
   Received the gift divine,
And still that light she lifteth
   O'er all the Earth to shine.
It is the golden casket
   Where gems of truth are stored,
It is the heaven-drawn picture
   Of Thee, the living Word.

3 It floateth like a banner
   Before God's host unfurled,
It shineth like a beacon
   Above the darkling world,
It is the chart and compass,
   That o'er life's surging sea,
'Mid mists and rocks and quicksands,
   Still guides, O Christ, to Thee.

The Holy Ghost.

4 Oh make Thy Church, dear Saviour,
A lamp of burnished gold,
To bear before the nations
Thy true light, as of old.
Oh teach Thy wandering pilgrims
By this their path to trace,
Till, clouds and darkness ended,
They see Thee face to face.

103   O God, O Spirit, Light of all that live.

10.10.10.10.10.10.   *"A habitation of God in the Spirit."*   Affiance.

Ger. GERHARD TERSTEEGEN, 1731.
Tr. CATH. WINKWORTH, 1855. *Abr.*   JOSEPH BARNBY, 1872.

1. { O God, O Spir-it, Light of all that live, Who dost on us that sit in dark-ness shine, }
{ Our darkness ev - er with Thy light doth strive; In vain Thou lur-est with Thy beams di - vine: }

Yet none, O Spir - it, from Thine eye can hide; Glad-ly will I Thy searching glance a - bide.

2 Search all my hidden parts, whate'er impure
Thy light discovers there, do Thou destroy;
The bitt'rest pain I willingly endure,
Such pain is followed by eternal joy.
O Breath! from out th'eternal silence blow,
The precious fulness of my God bestow!

104   Our blest Redeemer, ere He breathed.

8.6.8.4.   *"I will not leave you orphans."*   **St. Cuthbert.**
HARRIET AUBER, 1829. *Abr.*   JOHN B. DYKES, 1860.

1. OUR blest Re-deem-er, ere He breath'd His ten-der last fare-well, A Guide, a

Com-fort-er, bequeath'd, With us to dwell.

2 He came sweet influence to impart,
   A gracious, willing guest,
   While He can find one humble heart
   Wherein to rest.

3 And His that gentle voice we hear,
   Soft as the breath of even,
   That checks each fault, calms every fear,
   And speaks of Heav'n.

4 And every virtue we possess,
   And every conquest won,
   And every thought of holiness,—
   Are His alone.

5 Spirit of purity and grace,
   Our weakness, pitying, see;
   Oh, make our hearts Thy dwelling-place,
   And worthier Thee.

105   Thy home is with the humble, Lord!

C. M.   *"The Lord is that Spirit."*   **Meditation.**
FREDERICK W. FABER, 1849. *Abr.*   SAMUEL P. TUCKERMAN, 1843. *Arr.* B. C. B.

1. THY home is with the hum-ble, Lord! The sim-plest are the best;

The Holy Ghost.

Thy lodg-ing is in child - like hearts; Thou mak - est there Thy rest.

2 Dear Comforter! Eternal Love!
   If Thou wilt stay with me,
   Of lowly thoughts and simple ways,
   I'll build a house for Thee.

3 Who made this breathing heart of mine
   But Thou, my heavenly Guest?
   Let no one have it then but Thee,
   And let it be Thy rest!

106   Fountain of Love! Thyself true God!

C. M.   *" My sighing is not hid from Thee."*   Xavier.
FREDERICK W. FABER, 1849. *Abr.*   JOHN STAINER, 1875.

1 FOUNTAIN of Love! Thyself true God!
   Who thro eternal days
   From Father and from Son hast flowed
   In uncreated ways!

2 Fixt in the Godhead's awful light
   Thy fiery Breath doth move.
   Thou art a wonder by Thyself,
   To worship and to love.

3 Ocean, wide-flowing Ocean Thou,
   Of uncreated Love!
   I tremble as within my soul
   I feel Thy waters move.

4 Thou art a Sea without a shore,
   Awful, immense, Thou art,
   A Sea which can contract itself
   Within my narrow heart.

5 And yet Thou art a Haven too,
   Out on the shoreless sea,
   A Harbor that can hold full well
   Shipwrecked humanity!

6 O Spirit, beautiful and dread!
   My comfort this shall be,
   That when I serve my dearest Lord
   That service worships Thee.

107   Our God, our God, Thou shinest here.

C. M.   *"Come from the four winds, O Breath!"*   **Marlow.**

THOMAS H. GILL, 1846. *Abr.*   JOHN CHETHAM, 1718. *Abr.*

1. Orn God, our God, Thou shin-est here, Thine own this lat - ter day; To us Thy ra - diant

steps ap-pear; We watch Thy glo- rious way.

2 Not only olden ages felt
    The presence of the Lord;
Not only with the fathers dwelt
    Thy Spirit and Thy word.

3 Doth not the Spirit still descend,
    And bring the heavenly fire?
Doth not He still the Church extend,
    And waiting souls inspire?

4 Come, Holy Ghost, in us arise;
    Be this Thy mighty hour;
And make Thy willing people wise
    To know Thy day of power!

5 Pour down Thy fire in us to glow,
    Thy might in us to dwell;
Again Thy works of wonder show,
    Thy blessèd secrets tell!

108   Enthroned on high, Almighty Lord!

C. M.   *"Thro Him we have our access, in one Spirit, unto the Father."*   **Kabzeel.**

THOMAS HAWEIS, 1792. *Abr.*   JOHANN G. C. STÖRL, 1744.

1. ENTHRONED on high, Al-might - y Lord! Thy Ho - ly Ghost send down. Ful - fill in us Thy

The Holy Ghost.

faith - ful word, And all Thy mercies crown.

2 Tho on our heads no tongues of fire
   Their wondrous powers impart,
   Grant, Saviour, what we more desire,
   Thy Spirit in our heart.

3 His love within us shed abroad,
   Life's ever-springing well,
   Till God in us, and we in God,
   In love eternal dwell.

109   He's come! let every knee be bent.

C. M.   *" The Spirit of adoption, whereby we cry, Abba."*   **Westminster.**
ARTHUR BEDFORD (?), 1733 *Abr.*   JAMES TURLE, 1843.

1. He's come! let ev - ery knee be bent, All hearts new joys re - sume!

Let na - tions sing with one con - sent, The Com - fort - er is come!

2 There is no end of the content
   And joy the Spirit brings;
Happy the man to whom 'tis lent!
   That man sees wondrous things.

3 Hail, blessèd Spirit! not a soul
   But doth Thy goodness feel;
Thou dost our darling sins control,
   And fix our wavering zeal.

4 As pilots by the compass steer
   Till they their harbor find,
So do Thy sacred breathings here
   Guide every wandering mind.

5 The flesh may strive our course t'im-
   The world's rough billows roar, [peach,
But by Thy help we're sure to reach
   The safe eternal shore.

110 Oh may Thy Spirit guide my feet.

C. M.

" Oh that there were such an heart in them !"

St. Martin's.

Isaac Watts, 1709. 1719. Arr.

William Tansur, 1735.

1. On may Thy Spir - - it guide my feet, In ways of righteous - ness;

Make ev - ery path of du - ty straight And plain be - fore my face.

2 Lord! search my thoughts, and try my ways,
And make my soul sincere;
Then shall I stand before Thy face,
And find acceptance there.

111 Holy Ghost, with light divine.

7.7.7.7.

"A lamp shining in a dark place until the day dawn."

Immanuel.

Andrew Reed, 1825.

Richard Redhead, 1852.

1. Ho - ly Ghost, with light di - vine, Shine up - on this heart of mine. Chase the shades of
2. Ho - ly Ghost, with light di - vine, Cleanse this guilty heart of mine; Long hath sin, with -

night away, Turn my darkness into day.
out control, Held dominion o'er my soul. *Amen.*

3 Holy Ghost, with joy divine,
Cheer this saddened heart of mine.
Bid my many woes depart,
Heal my wounded, bleeding heart.

4 Holy Spirit, all divine,
Dwell within this heart of mine.
Cast down every idol-throne.
Reign supreme and reign alone! *Amen.*

112   O God of truth, whose living word.

C. M.   *"Thy word is truth."*   **St. Stephen.**

THOMAS HUGHES, 1859. *Abr.*   WILLIAM JONES, 1789.

1. O God of truth, whose liv - ing word   Up - holds what - e'er hath breath,

Look down on Thy cre - a - tion, Lord, En - slaved by sin and death.

2 Set up Thy standard, Lord, that we,
Who claim a heavenly birth,
May march with Thee to smite the lies
That vex Thy groaning Earth.

3 *We* fight for truth, *we* fight for God,
Poor slaves of lies and sin!
He who would fight for Thee on Earth
Must first be true within.

4 Thou God of truth, for whom we long,
Thou who wilt hear our prayer,
Do Thine own battle in our hearts,
And slay the falsehood there.

5 Yea, come! then tried as in the fire,
From every lie set free,
Thy perfect truth shall dwell in us,
And we shall live in Thee.

113   All hail the power of Jesus' Name.

C. M.   *" Behold the Man !"*   **Miles Lane.**

EDWARD PERRONET, 1779.
(The unchanged original text.)

WILLIAM SHRUBSOLE, 1779.
Har. JOHN B. DYKES, 1861.

1. ALL hail the pow'r of Je - sus' Name! Let an - gels prostrate fall! Bring forth the roy-al

di - a - dem, To CROWN HIM! CROWN HIM! CROWN HIM! CROWN HIM LORD OF ALL!

2 Let high-born seraphs tune the lyre,
　　And, as they tune it, fall
　Before His face who tunes their choir,
　　And crown Him Lord of all.

3 Crown Him, ye morning stars of light!
　　Who fixt this floating ball;
　Now hail the Strength of Israel's might,
　　And crown Him Lord of all!

4 Crown Him, ye martyrs of your God,
　　Who from His altar call;
　Extol the Stem of Jesse's rod,
　　And crown Him Lord of all.

5 Ye seed of Israel's chosen race,
　　Ye ransomed of the fall,
　Hail Him who saves you by His grace,
　　And crown Him Lord of all.

6 Hail Him, ye heirs of David's line,
　　Whom David Lord did call,
　The God incarnate, Man divine,
　　And crown Him Lord of all.

7 Sinners! whose love can ne'er forget
　　The wormwood and the gall,
　Go spread your trophies at His feet
　　And crown Him Lord of all.

8 Let every tribe and every tongue
　That bound Creation's call,
　Now shout in universal song,
　The crownèd Lord of all.

114   The Head that once was crowned with thorns.

C. M.   *" Far be it from me to glory save in the Cross of our Lord Jesus Christ."*   **Coronation.**

THOMAS KELLY, 1820. *Abr.*   OLIVER HOLDEN, 1792.

1. THE Head that once was crown'd with thorns, Is crown'd with glory now; A roy-al di - a - dem a-

dorns the might-y Vic - tor's brow; A roy-al di - a - dem a-dorns The mighty Vic - tor's brow.

2 The joy of all who dwell above,
    The joy of all below,
To whom He manifests His love,
    And grants His name to know.

3 The Cross He bore is life and health,
    Tho shame and death to Him;
His people's hope, His people's wealth,
    Their everlasting theme.

115   Crown Him with many crowns.

S. M.   *" Let all the angels of God worship Him."*   **Sunderland.**

MATTHEW BRIDGES, 1847. *Abr.*   HENRY SMART, 1868.

1. CROWN Him with many crowns,
    The Lamb upon His throne ;   Hark! how the heav'nly anthem drowns
                                     All mu-sic but its own!

2 His reign shall know no end,
    And round His piercèd feet
Fair flowers of Paradise extend
    Their fragrance ever sweet.

3 Awake, my soul! and sing
    Of Him who died for Thee,
And hail Him as the matchless King,
    Thro all eternity.

116 Immortal Love! forever full.

C. M.   *"One is your Master, even the Christ."*   **St. Peter.**

JOHN G. WHITTIER, 1867. *Abr.*   ALEXANDER R. REINAGLE, 1826.

1. Im - mor - tal Love, for - ev - er full, For - ev - er flow - ing free,

For - ev - er shared, for - ev - er whole, A nev - er - ebb - ing Sea!

2 Our outward lips confess the name
   All other names above ;
   Love only knoweth whence it came
   And comprehendeth Love.

3 Blow, winds of God, awake and blow
   The mists of Earth away!
   Shine out, O Light Divine, and show
   How wide and far we stray!

4 We may not climb the heavenly steeps
   To bring the Lord Christ down,
   In vain we search the lowest deeps
   For Him no depths can drown.

5 In joy of inward peace, or sense
   Of sorrow over sin,
   He is His own best evidence,
   His Witness is within.

6 Yea, warm, sweet, tender, even yet
   A present help is He ;
   And faith has still its Olivet,
   And love its Galilee.

7 O Love! O Life! Our faith and sight
   Thy presence maketh one,
   As thro transfigured clouds of white
   We trace the noonday Sun.

8 So, to our mortal eyes subdued,
   Flesh-veiled but not concealed,
   We know in Thee the Fatherhood
   And heart of God revealed.

9 Apart from Thee all gain is loss,
   All labor vainly done ;
   The solemn shadow of Thy Cross
   Is better than the Sun!

10 Thou judgest us. Thy purity
   Doth all our lusts condemn;
   The love that draws us nearer Thee
   Is hot with wrath to them.

11 Our Friend, our Brother, and our Lord,
   What may Thy service be?
   Nor name nor form nor ritual word:
   But simply following Thee.

117   When morning gilds the skies.

6.6.6.6.6.6.   *" Singing, with grace in your hearts, to the Lord."*   **Laudes Domini.**

EDWARD CASWALL, 1849. *Abr.*   JOSEPH BARNBY, 1868.

1. When morn-ing gilds the skies, My heart a - wak-ing cries May Je - sus Christ be praised.

A - like at work and prayer To Je - sus I re - pair; May Je - sus Christ be praised.

2 Whene'er the sweet church-bell
   Peals over hill and dell,
   May Jesus Christ be praised.
   Oh, hark to what it sings!
   As joyously it rings,
   May Jesus Christ be praised.

3 To Thee, O God above,
   I cry with glowing love;
   May Jesus Christ be praised.
   When evil thoughts molest,
   With this I shield my breast,
   May Jesus Christ be praised.

4 Does sadness fill my mind?
   A solace here I find,
   May Jesus Christ be praised.
   Or fades my earthly bliss?
   My comfort still is this,
   May Jesus Christ be praised.

5 Be this, while life is mine,
   My canticle divine,
   May Jesus Christ be praised;
   And when this life is gone,
   Thro all the ages on,
   May Jesus Christ be praised.

Praise to Christ.

118 Majestic sweetness sits enthroned.

C. M. *" I rejoice at Thy word as one that findeth great spoil."* **Ortonville.**

SAMUEL STENNETT, 1787. *Abr.* THOMAS HASTINGS, 1837.

1. Ma - jes - tic sweetness sits enthroned Up - on the Saviour's brow; His head with

radiant glories crowned, His lips with grace o'er - flow,— His lips with grace o'er - flow.

2 No mortal can with Him compare
Among the sons of men;
Fairer is He than all the fair
That fill the heavenly train.

3 He saw me plunged in deep distress,
He flew to my relief.

For me He bore the shameful Cross,
And carried all my grief.

4 Since from Thy bounty I receive
Such proofs of love divine,
Had I a thousand hearts to give,
Lord, they should all be Thine!

119 These eyes, O Jesus! ne'er have seen.

C. M. *" A little while and ye shall see Me."* **Bedford.**

RAY PALMER, 1857. *Abr.* WILLIAM WHEALL, 1720.

1. These eyes, O Je-sus, ne'er have seen That ra - diant form of Thine. The veil of sense hangs

Praise to Christ.

2 Yet, tho I have not seen, and still
   Must rest in faith alone,
I love Thee, dearest Lord! and will,
   Unseen, but not unknown.

3 When death these mortal eyes shall seal,
   And still this throbbing heart,
The rending veil shall Thee reveal,
   All glorious as Thou art!

dark be-tween Thy blessèd face and mine.

120   Ye servants of God! your Master proclaim.

5.5.5.6, D.   *" He is apparelled with majesty." -*   **Lyons.**

CHARLES WESLEY, 1744. *Abr.*   FRANCIS JOSEPH HAYDN, 1770.

Forte.

1. Ye serv-ants of God! Your Mas-ter pro-claim, And pub-lish a-broad His won-der-ful name.

maestoso.

The name, all-vic-torious, Of Je-sus ex - tol; His kingdom is glorious, And rules o-ver all.

2 God ruleth on high,
   Almighty to save;
   And still He is nigh;
   His presence we have.
The great congregation
   His triumph shall sing,
Ascribing salvation
   To Jesus, our King.

3 Then let us adore,
   And give Him His right,
   All glory, and power,
   And wisdom and might,
All honor and blessing,
   With angels above,
And thanks never ceasing,
   And infinite love.

121 Fairest Lord Jesus.

5.6.8.5.5.8. "*He showeth Himself thro the lattice.*" Crusader's Hymn.
ANON, 12th Century, A. D. Har. RICHARD S. WILLIS, 1847.

1. FAIREST Lord Je - sus, Ru - ler of all na - ture, O Thou of God and man the Son;

Thee will I cher - ish, Thee will I hon-or, Thou, my soul's glo - ry, joy and crown!

2 Fair are the meadows,
Fairer still the woodlands,
Robed in the blooming garb of spring:
Jesus is fairer,
Jesus is purer,
Who makes the woful heart to sing.

3 Fair is the sunshine,
Fairer still the moonlight,
And all the twinkling starry host.
Jesus shines brighter,
Jesus shines purer,
Than all the angels Heaven can boast.

122 How sweet the name of Jesus sounds!

"*Whose house are we if we hold fast our boldness, and the glorying of our hope firm unto the end!*"

C. M. Bristol.
JOHN NEWTON, 1779. Abr. EDWARD HODGES, 1846.

1. How SWEET the name of Je-sus sounds, In a be - liev - er's ear! It soothes his sor - rows,

Praise to Christ.

2 It makes the wounded spirit whole,
   And calms the troubled breast;
   'Tis Manna to the hungry soul,
   And, to the weary, Rest.

3 Weak is the effort of my heart,
   And cold my warmest thought;
   But when I see Thee as Thou art,
   I'll praise Thee as I ought.

heals his wounds, And drives away his fear.

123   My God, I love Thee! not because.

C. M.   *"He hath clothed me with the garments of salvation."*   **Würtemburg.**

Lat. FRANCIS XAVIER, 1542.
Tr. EDWARD CASWALL, 1849.

JOHANN GEORG FRECH, 1844.

1. My God, I love Thee! not be - cause I hope for Heav'n there - by;
2. Thou, O my Je - sus, Thou didst me Up - on the Cross em - brace;

Nor yet be - cause, if I love not, I must for - ev - er die.
For me didst bear the nails and spear, And man - i - fold dis - grace,

3 And griefs and torments numberless,
   And sweat of agony,
   Yea, death itself; and all for one
   Who was Thine enemy!

4 Then why, O blessèd Jesus Christ,
   Should I not love Thee well!
   Not for the sake of winning Heaven,
   Nor of escaping Hell;—

5 Not with the hope of gaining aught,
   Not seeking a reward:
   But, as Thyself hast lovèd me,
   O ever-loving Lord!

6 E'en so I love Thee, and will love
   And in Thy praise will sing;
   Solely because Thou art my God
   And my Eternal King.

124 O Thou great Friend to all the sons of men.

10.10.10.10.   *"He could not be hid!"*   **Cassidy.**

THEODORE PARKER, 1846.   HUBERT P. MAIN, 1895.

1. O Thou great Friend to all the sons of men, Who once didst come in humblest guise below,

Sin to re-buke, To break the captive's chain, And call Thy brethren forth from want and woe:—

Copyright, 1896, by Hubert P. Main.

2 We look to Thee; Thy truth is still the light
   Which guides the nations, groping on their way,
   Stumbling and falling in disastrous night,
   Yet hoping ever for the perfect day.

3 Yes! Thou art still the Life; Thou art the Way
   The holiest know; Light, Life, and Way of Heaven!
   And they who dearest hope and deepest pray,
   Toil by the Light, Life, Way, which Thou hast given.

125   In the Cross of Christ I glory.

8.7.8.7.   *"Be of good cheer, I have overcome the world."*   **Rathbun.**

JOHN BOWRING, 1825.   ITHAMAR CONKEY, 1847.

Used by per. O. Ditson Co.

Grace.

1 In the Cross of Christ I glory,
   Tow'ring o'er the wrecks of time;
   All the light of sacred story
   Gathers round its head sublime.

2 When the woes of life o'ertake me,
   Hopes deceive and fears annoy,
   Never shall the Cross forsake me;
   Lo! it glows with peace and joy.

3 When the sun of bliss is beaming
   Light and love upon my way,
   From the Cross the radiance streaming
   Adds new lustre to the day.

4 Bane and blessing, pain and pleasure,
   By the Cross are sanctified;
   Peace is there that knows no measure,
   Joys that thro all time abide.

126   Weary of Earth and laden with my sin.

10.10.10.10.   *" I came to call sinners."*   **Langran.**
SAMUEL J. STONE, 1865. *Abr.*   JAMES LANGRAN, 1863.

1. Wea-ry of Earth and lad-en with my sin, I look at Heav'n and long to en-ter in:

But there no e-vil thing may find a home: And yet I hear a Voice that bids me "*Come.*"

2 It is the voice of Jesus that I hear.
   His are the hands stretch'd out to draw me near.
   And His the blood that can for all atone,
   And set me faultless there before the throne.

3 Yea, Thou wilt answer for me, righteous Lord!
   Thine all the merit, mine the great reward;
   Thine the sharp thorns, and mine the golden crown;
   Mine the life won, and Thine the life laid down.

127 Take up the cross, the Saviour said.

L. M. " *Let him take hold of My strength.*" **Samson.**

CHARLES WILLIAM EVEREST, 1833. *Abr.* GEORGE FRIDERIC HANDEL, 1741.

1. "TAKE up thy cross (the Sav - iour said), If thou wouldst My dis - ci - ple be;

De - ny thy - self, the world for - sake, And hum - bly fol - low aft - er Me."

2 Take up thy cross; let not its weight
Fill thy weak soul with vain alarm;
His strength shall bear thy spirit up,
And brace thy heart, and nerve thy arm.

3 Take up thy cross, and follow on,
Nor think till death to lay it down;
For only he who bears the cross
May hope to wear the glorious crown.

128 To-day the Saviour calls.

6.4.6.4. " *Whosoever will, let him come.*" **To-Day.**

SAMUEL FRANCIS SMITH, and
THOMAS HASTINGS, 1831. LOWELL MASON, 1831.

1. To - day the Saviour calls; Ye wand'rers, come! O ye be-night-ed souls, Why longer roam?

2 To-day the Saviour calls;
Oh, listen now!
Within these sacred walls
To Jesus bow.

3 The Spirit calls to-day;
Yield to His power!
Oh, grieve Him not away;
'Tis mercy's hour.

129   Behold, a Stranger's at the door!

L. M   *" And they were all astonished at the majesty of God."*   **Bera.**

JOSEPH GRIGG, 1765. *Abr.*   JOHN EDGAR GOULD, 1849.

1. BE-HOLD, a Stran-ger's at the door! He gen-tly knocks, has knocked be - fore;

Hath wait - ed long, is wait - ing still; You treat no oth - er friend so ill.

2 Oh, lovely attitude! He stands
With melting heart and loaded hands:
Oh, matchless kindness! and He shows
This matchless kindness to His foes.

3 If thou art poor, and poor thou art,
Lo He has riches to impart!
Yet know, nor of the terms complain,
If Jesus comes, He comes to reign.

130   Oh, cease, my wandering soul.

S. M.   *" I flee unto Thee to hide me."*   **St. Bride.**

WILLIAM A. MUHLENBERG, 1826. *Abr.*   SAMUEL HOWARD, 1762.

1 OH, cease, my wand'ring soul, On rest-less wing to roam; All the wide world, to ei-ther pole, Hath not for thee a home.

2 Behold the Ark of God!
Behold the open door!
Hasten to gain that dear abode,
And rove, my soul, no more.

3 There safe thou shalt abide;
There sweet shall be thy rest;
And every longing satisfied,
With full salvation blest.

131   I bore with thee long weary days and nights.

Chant.   *" The love of Christ which passeth knowledge."*   **Troyte's Chant.**
CHRISTINA G. ROSSETTI, 1856.   Arr. ARTHUR H. D. TROYTE, 1857.

1 I BORE with thee long weary | days and | nights, ||
   Thro many pangs of heart, thro | many | tears, ||
   I bore with thee, thy hardness, | coldness, | slights, ||
   For three and | thirty | years. ||

2 Who else had dared for thee what | I have | dared? ||
   I plunged the depth most deep from | bliss a- | bove ;
   I not My flesh, I not My | spirit | spared ; ||
   Give thou Me | love for | love! ||

3 For thee I thirsted in the | daily | drouth, ||
   For thee I trembled in the | nightly | frost. ||
   Much sweeter thou than | honey " to My | mouth ;
   Why wilt thou | still be | lost? ||

4 I bore thee on My shoulders, | and re- | joiced. ||
   Men only marked upon My | shoulders | borne ||
   The branding Cross, and | shouted hungry- | voiced, ||
   Or wagged their | heads in | scorn. ||

5 Thee did nails grave upon My | hands.   Thy | name ||
   Did thorns for frontlets stamp be- | tween Mine | eyes.||
   I, Holy One, put on thy | guilt and | shame ;— ||
   I, God, Priest, | Sacri- | fice. ||

6 A thief upon My right hand | and My | left. ||
   Six hours alone, athirst, in | mise- | ry,— ||
   At length in death one smote My | heart, and ' cleft ||
   A hiding- | place for | thee! ||

7 Nailed to the racking Cross, than | bed of | down ||
   More dear, whereon to stretch My- | self and | sleep, ||
   So did I win a Kingdom— | share My | crown! ||
   A harvest— | come and | reap! ||

Grace.

132   O Jesus, Thou art standing.

7s & 6s, D.   *"Behold, I stand at the door and knock."*   **Clare.**

WILLIAM W. HOW, 1854.   HUBERT P. MAIN, 1877.

1. O Je - sus, Thou art stand - ing Out -side the fast-closed door, In low - ly pa-tience

wait - ing To pass the thresh-old o'er; Shame on us, Christian breth - ren, His

name and sign who bear, Oh, shame, thrice shame up - on us, To keep Him standing there!

2 O Jesus, Thou art knocking,
    And lo! that hand is scarred,
And thorns Thy brow encircle,
    And tears Thy face have marred.
Oh, love that passeth knowledge,
    So patiently to wait!
Oh sin that hath no equal,
    So fast to bar the gate!

3 O Jesus, Thou art pleading
    In accents meek and low,
'I died for you, My children,
    And will ye treat Me so?'
O Lord, with shame and sorrow
    We open now the door:
Dear Saviour, enter, enter,
    And leave us nevermore!

133 Lift up your heads, ye mighty gates.

L. M.   *"Let us lift up our heart with our hands."*   **Anastasius.**

Ger. George Weissel, 1635.
Tr. Cath. Winkworth, 1855. *Abr.*

Johann A. Freylinghausen, 1704. *Abr.*

1. Lift up your heads, ye might-y gates; Be-hold the King of glo-ry waits!

The King of kings is draw-ing near, The Sav-iour of the world is here.

2 Oh, blest the land, the city blest,
Where Christ, the Ruler is confest!
Oh, happy hearts and happy homes,
To whom this King of triumph comes!

3 Redeemer! come; I open wide
My heart to Thee. Here, Lord, abide.
Let me Thine inner presence feel,
Thy grace and love in me reveal.

134 Thy grace is all of grace!

6.6.8.4.   *"He came and preached peace to you that were far off."*   **Via Pacis.**

M. W. S., 1836.

Joseph Barnby, 1872.

1. Thy grace is all of grace, Thou Mer-ci-ful and Just! The light that shines in

Grace.

Je - sus' face Is all my trust

And placed my perilled feet within
 Life's narrow way.

3 From God no more estranged,
 In Christ's dear blood made nigh,
Mine alienage forever changed,
 A child am I.

4 Thro Love's unearned release,
 Submissive at Thy side,
Thou, Lord, my Righteousness and Peace,
 My heart dost guide.

2 It found me in my sin,
 Will-driven and wide astray,

135 "Art thou weary, art thou languid?"

8.5.8.3.   *"Let no man rob you of your prize."*   Welcome.

Gk. Stephen, The Sabaite, cir. 750.
Tr. John M. Neale, 1851.   Ethelbert W. Bullinger, 1876.

1. Art thou wea - ry, art thou lan - guid? Art thou sore dis - trest? "Come to Me," saith

One, "and com - ing, Be ...... at rest!"

4 If I find Him, if I follow,
 What His guerdon here?
"Many a sorrow, many a labor,
 Many a tear."

5 If I still hold closely to Him,
 What hath He at last?
"Sorrow vanquished, labor ended,
 Jordan past."

2 Hath He marks to lead me to Him,
 If He be my Guide?
"In His feet and hands are wound-prints,
 And His side."

3 Is there diadem, as Monarch,
 That His brow adorns?
"Yea, a crown in very surety,
 But of thorns."

6 If I ask Him to receive me,
 Will He say me nay?
"Not till Earth, and not till Heaven
 Pass away!"

7 Finding, following, keeping, struggling,
 Is He sure to bless?
Saints, apostles, prophets, martyrs,
 Answer, Yes!

136   The Lord is rich and merciful.

C. M.   "*A better covenant, which hath been enacted upon better promises.*"   **Canterbury.**

THOMAS TOKE LYNCH, 1850. *Abr.*   EDWARD BLANCKS, 1592.

1. The Lord is rich and mer - ci - ful, The Lord is ve - ry kind;

Oh come to Him, come now to Him, With a be - liev - ing mind.

137

2 His comforts they shall strengthen thee,
    Like flowing waters cool,
And He shall for thy spirit be
    A fountain ever full.

3 He shall be to thee like the sea,
    And thou shalt surely feel
His wind, that bloweth healthfully,
    Thy sicknesses to heal.

4 The Lord is wonderful and wise,
    As all the ages tell;
Oh learn of Him, learn now of Him,
    Then with thee it is well.

5 And with His light thou shalt be blest,
    Therein to work and live;
And He shall be to thee a rest
    When evening hours arrive.

1 ALMIGHTY and Most Merciful,
    Our Father, we have erred,
And, from Thy way, like sheep, astray,
    Have our desires preferred.

2 We have offended Thy good laws,
    Misdeeds have done, and thus
The things we ought we have not wrought,
    There is no health in us.

3 But have Thou mercy still on those
    To penitence restored;
Thou hast declared they shall be spared,
    Thro Jesus Christ our Lord.

4 And, for His sake, a godly life
    Most mercifully give,
That in the same to Thy dear name
    Hereafter we may live.

M. W. S., 1892.

Grace.

138   Out of the depths of woe.

S. M.   *"Before I was afflicted I went astray."*   **Deliverance.**

JAMES MONTGOMERY, 1822. *Abr.*   SAMUEL SED. WESLEY, 1863. *Abr.*

1. OUT of the depths of woe, To Thee, O Lord, I cry! Darkness surrounds me: but I know That Thou art ev-er nigh.

2 I cast my hope on Thee;
Thou canst, Thou wilt forgive;
Wert Thou to mark iniquity,
Who in Thy sight could live?

3 Humbly on Thee I wait,
Confessing all my sin.
Lord! I am knocking at Thy gate;
Open, and take me in.

139   Amazing grace! how sweet the sound.

C. M.   *"That in me as chief might Jesus Christ shew forth all His long suffering."*   **Obedience.**

JOHN NEWTON, 1779.   PHILADELPHIA CHORALBUCH, 1813.

1. A - MAZ - ING grace! how sweet the sound That sav'd a wretch like me! I once was lost: but

now am found.—Was blind: but now I see.

2 'Twas grace that taught my heart to fear,
And grace my fears relieved;

How precious did that grace appear,
The hour I first believed!

3 Thro many dangers, toils, and snares,
I have already come;
'Tis grace hath brought me safe thus far,
And grace will lead me home.

4 The Lord hath promised good to me,
His word my hope secures;
He will my Shield and Portion be,
So long as life endures.

140   From the recesses of a lowly spirit.

11.11.11.5.   **Chant.**   *"That which I see not, teach Thou me."*   **Gould's Chant.**

JOHN BOWRING, 1823.   JOHN EDGAR GOULD, 1845.

1. From the recesses of a lowly spirit, Our humble prayer ascends. O | Fa - ther | hear it ! ||

Borne on the trembling wings of.... | fear · and | meekness,|| For - | give · its | weakness.

2 We know, we feel, how mean and how unworthy
The lowly sacrifice we | pour · be- | fore Thee;— ||
What can we offer Thee,—O | Thou · most | holy !— ||
But | sin · and | folly?

3 Lord! in Thy sight, who every bosom viewest,
Cold are our warmest vows, and | vain our | truest; ||
Thoughts of a hurrying hour—our | lips re- | peat them,— ||
Our | hearts · for- | get them.

4 We see Thy hand—it leads us, it supports us.
We hear Thy voice—it | counsels · and it | courts us;— ||
And then we turn away!—and | still · Thy | kindness ||
For- | gives · our | blindness.

5 Father and Saviour! plant within each bosom
The seeds of holiness, and | bid them | blossom ||
In fragrance and in beauty | bright and | vernal, ||
And | spring e- | ternal.

Contrition.

141 O Thou Shepherd of Thine Israel, hear us!

10.9.10.9. *"The Lord of peace Himself give you peace at all times, in all ways."* **Zuriel.**

Psalm Lxxx.
M. Woolsey Stryker, 1883.

Joseph Barnby, 1869.

1. O Thou Shepherd of Thine Israel, hear us! Thou that Joseph like a flock dost lead,

From the cher-u - bim shine forth and cheer us, Stir Thy strength and come to help our need.

2 Wilt Thou hear Thy people's prayer with anger,
  Measure them the bread and drink of tears,
  Visit strife and scorn upon our languor,
  Grant no more the grace of other years?

3 Shall the goodly vine that Thou didst cherish,
  Once that grew and shaded all the hills,
  Break and waste and fall and burn and perish,
  While her ruin Thy rebuke fulfills?

4 Turn us, Lord, again! in mercy, hearken,
  All our waywardness and shame forgive.
  Leave us not unsought, while shadows darken:
  Cause Thy face to shine, and we shall live.

5 Look from Heaven, O God, when sorrows thicken,
  By Thy hand, once more, our strength maintain;
  We will call Thy name, if Thou but quicken,
  We will never leave Thy love again

Contrition.

142   With broken heart, and contrite sigh.

L. M.   *"I was wounded in the house of My friends."*   **Warner.**

CORNELIUS ELVEN, 1852. *Abr.*   GIOACCHIMO ROSSINI.
ARR. GEORGE KINGSLEY, 1853.

1. WITH bro-ken heart, and con-trite sigh, A tremb-ling sin - ner, Lord, I cry:
Thy pardoning grace is rich and free; O God, be mer - ci - ful to me.

2 I smite upon my troubled breast,
With deep and conscious guilt opprest,
Christ and His Cross my only plea;
O God, be merciful to me.

3 Far off I stand with tearful eyes,
Nor dare uplift them to the skies:
But Thou dost all my anguish see;
O God, be merciful to me.

143   Have mercy, Lord on me.

S. M.   *"Blot out my transgression."*   **Braden.**

TATE & BRADY, 1698. *Abr.*   WILLIAM B. BRADBURY, 1844.

1. HAVE mer-cy, Lord, on me, As Thou wert ever kind; Let me op-prest with loads of guilt, Thy wonted mercy find.

2 Against Thee, Lord, alone,
And only in Thy sight,
Have I transgressed; and tho condemned
Must own Thy judgments right.

3 Withdraw not Thou Thy help,
Nor cast me from Thy sight;
Nor let Thy Holy Spirit take
His everlasting flight!

Contrition.

144   When wounded sore, the stricken soul.

C. M.   *"I know their sorrows."*   **Manoah.**

CECIL F. ALEXANDER, 1858.   FRANZ J. HAYDN, 1801.
                                   ARR. HENRY W. GREATOREX, 1851.

1. When wound-ed sore, the strick-en soul Lies bleed-ing and un-bound,

One on-ly hand, a pierc-ed hand, Can heal the sin-ner's wound.

2 When sorrow swells the laden breast
   And tears of anguish flow,
   One only heart, a broken heart,
   Can feel the sinner's woe.

3 When penitence has wept in vain
   O'er some dark fouling spot,
   One only stream, a stream of blood,
   Can wash away the blot.

4 'Tis Jesus' blood that washes white,
   His hand that brings relief,
   His heart that's touched with all our joys,
   And feeleth for our grief.

5 Lift up Thy bleeding hand, O Lord,
   Unseal that cleansing tide;
   We have no shelter from our sin,
   But in Thy wounded side!

145

1 ALL that I was,—my sin, my guilt,
   My death, was all mine own;
   All that I am, I owe to Thee,
   My gracious God! alone.

2 The evil of my former state
   Was mine and only mine;
   The good in which I now rejoice,
   Is Thine and only Thine.

3 The darkness of my former state,
   The bondage, all was mine;
   The light of life in which I walk,
   The liberty, is Thine.

4 All that I am e'en here on Earth,
   All that I hope to be,
   When Jesus comes and glory dawns,
   I owe it, Lord! to Thee.

HORATIUS BONAR, 1850. *Abr.*

Contrition.

146 We have not known Thee as we ought.

L. M. *" Heal me, O Lord, and I shall be healed! save me, and I shall be saved!"* **Spires.**

THOMAS B. POLLOCK, 1889. *Abr.* MARTIN LUTHER, 1541.

1. WE have not known Thee as we ought, Nor learned Thy wis-dom, grace and power;

The things of Earth have filled our thought, And tri-fles of the pass-ing hour.

2 We have not feared Thee as we ought,
Nor bowed beneath Thine awful eye,
Nor guarded deed and word and thought,
Remembering that God was nigh.

3 We have not loved Thee as we ought,
Nor cared that we are loved by Thee;
Thy presence we have coldly sought,
And feebly longed Thy face to see.

4 We have not served Thee as we ought;
Alas! the duties left undone,
The work with little fervor wrought,
The battles lost, or scarcely won!

5 When shall we know Thee as we ought,
And fear and love and serve aright!
When shall we, out of trial brought,
Be perfect in the land of light!

147 Earth has a joy unknown to Heaven.

L. M. *" Having our hearts sprinkled from an evil conscience."* **Canonbury.**

ABRAHAM LUCAS HILLHOUSE, 1822. *Abr.* ROBERT SCHUMANN, 1839.

1. EARTH has a joy unknown to Heav'n,—The newborn peace of sins forgiv'n! Tears of such pure and

Faith.

deep delight, Ye angels! never dim'd your sight.

2 Loud is the song. The heavenly plain
Is shaken with the choral strain,
And dying echoes, floating far,
Draw music from each chiming star.

3 But I amid your choirs shall shine,
And all your knowledge shall be mine;
Ye on your harps must lean to hear
A secret chord that mine will bear!

148 My faith looks up to Thee.

6s & 4s. "*If righteousness is thro the law, then Christ died for naught.*" **Olivet.**

RAY PALMER, 1830. LOWELL MASON, 1832.

1. My faith looks up to Thee, Thou Lamb of Cal - va - ry, Sav - iour di - vine! Now hear me

while I pray, Take all my guilt a - way, Oh, let me, from this day, Be who - ly Thine.

2 May Thy rich grace impart,
Strength to my fainting heart,
My zeal inspire.
As Thou hast died for me,
Oh! may my love to Thee
Pure, warm, and changeless be,
A living fire!

3 While life's dark maze I tread,
And griefs around me spread,
Be Thou my Guide.
Bid darkness turn to day,

Wipe sorrow's tears away,
Nor let me ever stray
From Thee aside.

4 When ends life's transient dream,
When death's cold, sullen stream
Shall o'er me roll,
Blest Saviour! then, in love,
Fear and distrust remove;
Oh! bear me safe above,
A ransomed soul!

149   Rock, of Ages, cleft for me.

7.7.7.7.7.7.   *" I have laid help upon One that is mighty."*   **Rock of Ages.**

AUGUSTUS M. TOPLADY, 1776.   JOHN B. DYKES, 1871. *All.*

1. Rock of A - ges, cleft for me, Let me hide my - self in Thee!

Let the wa - ter and the blood, From Thy riv - en side which flowed,

Be of sin the dou - ble cure, Cleanse me from its guilt and power.

2 Not the labors of my hands
Can fulfill Thy law's demands;
Could my zeal no respite know,
Could my tears for ever flow,—
All for sin could not atone;
Thou must save, and Thou alone!

3 Nothing in my hand I bring;
Simply to Thy Cross I cling;
Naked, come to Thee for dress,

Helpless, look to Thee for grace;
Foul, I to the fountain fly,
Wash me, Saviour! or I die.

4 While I draw this fleeting breath,
When mine eyelids close in death,
When I soar thro realms unknown,
See Thee on Thy judgment throne,
Rock of Ages, cleft for me,
Let me hide myself in Thee!

Faith.

150   I heard the voice of Jesus say.

C. M. D.   *" God is faithful, thro whom ye were called into the fellowship of His Son."* **Vox Dilecti.**

HORATIUS BONAR, 1850.   JOHN B. DYKES, 1868.

1. I HEARD the voice of Je - sus say, "Come un - to me and rest; Lay down, thou wea-ry one, lay down Thy head up - on my breast." I came to Je - sus as I was, Wea - ry, and worn, and sad: I found in Him a rest-ing-place, And He has made me glad.

2 I heard the voice of Jesus say,
     " Behold! I freely give
  The living-water ; thirsty one!
     Stoop down, and drink and live."
I came to Jesus, and I drank
     Of that life-giving stream ;
My thirst was quenched, my soul revived,
     And now I live in Him.

3 I heard the voice of Jesus say,
     " I am this dark world's light ;
  Look unto me ; thy morn shall rise,
     And all thy day be bright."
I looked to Jesus, and I found,
     In Him, my Star, my Sun ;
And in that light of life I'll walk,
     Till traveling days are done.

𝔉𝔞𝔦𝔱𝔥.

151   Slain for my soul, for all my sins defamed.

10.10.10.10.   *"Thou shalt be with Me."*   **Dalkeith.**

HERBERT KYNASTON, 1862. *Abr.*   THOMAS HEWLETT, 1863.

1. SLAIN for my soul, for all my sins defamed, King, crown'd with thorns, with blasphemies proclaim'd!
2. For Thy tor-men-tors, for my par-don, sue,—"Fa-ther, for-give; they know not what they do!"

High o'er the clouds Thy roy-al Sign I see; Throned on Thy glory, Lord, re-mem-ber me!
When they that pierc'd, when every eye, shall see Thee in Thy kingdom, Lord, remember me! A-men.

3 Mid all the thronging of Thy ransomed dead,
With all the Book of Life before Thee spread,
Toss'd, like a waif, upon the living sea
By angels parted, Lord, remember me! *Amen.*

152   Just as I am, without one plea.

L. M.   *"According to your faith be it unto you."*   **Woodworth.**

CHARLOTTE ELLIOTT, 1836.   WILLIAM B. BRADBURY, 1849.

1. JUST as I am, without one plea, But that Thy blood was shed for me, And that Thou bidd'st me come to

Faith.

Thee. O Lamb of God! I come—I come!

4 Just as I am, poor, wretched, blind;
Sight, riches, healing of the mind,
Yea, all I need in Thee to find,
O Lamb of God, I come—I come.

5 Just as I am Thou wilt receive,
Wilt welcome, pardon, cleanse, relieve!
Because, Thy promise I believe,
O Lamb of God, I come—I come.

2 Just as I am, and waiting not
To rid my soul of one dark blot, [spot,
To Thee, whose blood can cleanse each
O Lamb of God, I come—I come.

6 Just as I am; Thy love unknown
Hath broken every barrier down!
Now to be Thine, yea, Thine alone,
O Lamb of God, I come—I come.

3 Just as I am, tho tossed about
With many a conflict, many a doubt,
Fightings and fears within, without,
O Lamb of God, I come—I come.

7 Just as I am, of that free love [prove,
The breadth, length, depth, and height to
Here for a season, then above,
O Lamb of God, I come—I come.

153   Jesus, Saviour, pilot me.

7.7.7.7.7.7.   "Why are ye fearful?"   Pilot.
EDWARD HOPPER, 1871. Abr.   JOHN EDGAR GOULD, 1873.

1. Je - sus, Sav - iour, pi - lot me   O - ver life's tempestuous sea;   Un-known waves be-fore me
D.C.—Chart and com - pass came from Thee, Je - sus, Sav - iour, pi - lot me.

roll.   Hid-ing rock and treacherous shoal;

2 As a mother stills her child,
Thou canst hush the ocean wild;

Boisterous waves obey Thy will
When Thou say'st to them "Be still!"
Wondrous Sovereign of the sea!
Jesus, Saviour, pilot me.

3 When at last I near the shore,
And the fearful breakers roar
'Twixt me and the peaceful rest,
Then, while leaning on Thy breast,
May I hear Thee say to me,
"Fear not, I will pilot thee!"

ﬀaith.

154   A Tower of Refuge is our God!

8s, 7s & 6s, P.   "*Therefore will not we fear.*"   **"Ein' Feste Burg."**

Ger. Martin Luther, 1529.
Tr. M. W. S,, 1883. *Abr.*

Martin Luther, 1521.
Har. Hubert P. Main, 1881.

Forte.

1. { A Tower of Ref - uge is our God!—A good - ly ward and wea - pon.
{ He'll help us free, tho force or fraud To us may now mis - hap - pen.

That old Arch - en - e - my Would our un - do - ing be! Gross might and vast de -

vice His dread - ful ar - mor is; On Earth can none with - stand him!

2 By our might could we do no more
  Than vainly to have striven:
  But for us the right Man will war,
  Whom God Himself hath given.
  Dost ask who this can be?
  Christ Jesus, it is He!
  The Lord of Sabaoth,
  None other God, in troth.
  The field he holds forever.

3 For tho the world with demons swarmed,
  All minded to devour us,
  Not greatly were our souls alarmed;
  They cannot overpower us.
  This world's dark prince may still
  Lour sullen as he will;
  For he can harm us naught.
  'T is past. His doom is wrought.
  One word can bring his downfall!

155

Thy way, not mine, O Lord.

6.6.6.6, D.   *"If we ask anything according to His will He heareth us."*   **Baxter.**

HORATIUS BONAR, 1857. *Abr*   UZZIAH C. BURNAP, 1868.

1. THY way, not mine, O Lord, How - ev - er dark it be. Lead me by Thine own

hand, Choose out the path for me. Smooth let it be or rough, It will be

still the best; Wind-ing or straight, it leads Right on - ward to Thy rest. A - *men.*

2 I dare not choose my lot,
    I would not, if I might;
  Choose Thou for me, my God;
    So shall I walk aright.
  Take Thou my cup, and it
    With joy or sorrow fill,
  As best to Thee may seem.
    Choose Thou my good and ill.

3 Choose Thou for me my friends,
    My sickness or my health.
  Choose Thou my cares for me,
    My poverty or wealth.
  Not mine, not mine the choice,
    In things or great or small;
  Be Thou my Guide, my Strength,
    My Wisdom, and my All. *Amen.*

Faith.

156 Thro the love of God, our Saviour.

8.4.8.4.8.8.8.4. *" The angel of the Lord encampeth round about them that fear Him."*

MARY (BOWLY) PETERS, 1846.

All's Well.

JOSEPH BARNBY, 1875.

1. Thro the love of God, our Sav - iour, All will be well. Free and changeless

cres.

is His fa - vor. All, all is well. Precious is the blood that healed us; Per - fect

is the grace that sealed us; Strong the hand out-stretched to shield us; All must be well.

2 Tho we pass thro tribulation,
  All will be well;
Ours is such a full salvation,
  All, all is well.
Happy still in God confiding,
Fruitful, if in Christ abiding,
Holy, thro the Spirit's guiding,
  All must be well.

3 We expect a bright to-morrow;
  All will be well.
Faith can sing thro days of sorrow,
  All, all is well.
On our Father's love relying,
Jesus every need supplying,
Or in living, or in dying,
  All must be well.

157   From doubt and all its sullen pain.

L. M.   *" Behoved it not the Christ."*   **Redemption.**

M. W. S, 1890. *Abr.*   Luigi Cherubini, d. 1842.

1. From doubt and all its sul - len pain, From ev - 'ry wide, un - cer - tain quest,

My mind, O Christ, comes back a - gain, In Thee, the Word of God, to rest.

158

2 My laden conscience knows Thy voice,
  In Thee my reasonings end their strife,
  Thou strangely dost my heart rejoice;
  Where else is Way or Truth or Life?

3 Thou canst not disappoint the trust
  That finds its answers all in Thee;
  Because Thou wert the holy, just,
  And good,—and must forever be.

4 As we in God believe and dwell,
  So do we take Thy word and know
  That Love is Light, and all is well;
  Thou would'st have told were it not so!

5 O blessèd and enduring Rock,
  Who builds on Thee shall never fall!
  O Shepherd of one only flock,
  Beyond all fear enfold us all!

1 Oh grant us light, that we may know
  The wisdom Thou alone canst give,
  That truth may guide where'er we go,
  And virtue bless where'er we live.

2 Oh grant us light, that we may see
  Where error lurks in human lore,
  And turn our doubting mind to Thee,
  And love Thy simple Word the more.

3 Oh grant us light, that we may learn
  How dead is life from Thee apart,
  How sure is joy for all who turn
  To Thee an undivided heart.

4 Oh grant us light, in grief and pain,
  To lift our burdened hearts above,
  And count the very cross a gain,
  And bless our Father's hidden love.

Lawrence Tuttiett, 1864. *Abr.*

159 Lord, my weak thought in vain would climb.

L. M. *" Unto the upright there ariseth light in darkness."* **Melcombe.**

RAY PALMER, 1858. SAMUEL WEBBE, 1790.

1. LORD, my weak thought in vain would climb To search the star - ry vault pro - found;

In vain would wing her flight sub - lime, To find cre - a - tiou's out - most bound.

2 But weaker yet that thought must prove
To search Thy great eternal plan,—
Thy sovereign counsels, born of love
Long ages ere the world began!

3 When my dim reason would demand
Why that, or this, Thou dost ordain,
By some vast deep I seem to stand,
Whose secrets I must ask in vain.

4 When doubts disturb my troubled breast,
And all is dark as night to me,
Here, as on solid rock, I rest,—
That so it seemeth good to Thee!

5 Be this my joy, that evermore
Thou rulest all things at Thy will.
Thy sovereign wisdom I adore,
And calmly, sweetly, trust Thee still.

160

1 DEEP clouds Thy glorious throne infold;
Thou dost not yet make all things plain;
Nor could we now, our God, behold
The final issues of Thy reign.

2 But on the front of time and space
Thy burning prophecies appear,
Of vindicated truth and grace,
And love that casteth out all fear.

3 If now Thy reasons are concealed
And justice tarries on her way,
All will at last be well revealed,
And recompense the long delay.

4 Thou, Jesus Christ, hast entered there
Where cloudless light shines thro and [thro,
And we, to overcome, must share
Thy kingdom and Thy patience, too.

M. W. S., 1891.

161

O gift of gifts!

C. M. " And that not of yourselves." Dedham.

FREDERICK W. FABER, 1849. Abr. WILLIAM GARDINER, 1812.

1. O gift of gifts! O grace of Faith! My God, how can it be

That Thou, who hast dis - cern - ing love, Should'st give that gift to me!

162

2 How many hearts Thou mightst have had
More innocent than mine,
How many souls more worthy far
Of that sweet touch of Thine!

3 Ah, Grace, into unlikeliest hearts
It is Thy boast to come;
The glory of Thy light to find
In darkest spots a home.

4 The crowd of cares, the weightiest cross,
Seem trifles less than light;
Earth looks so little and so low
When faith shines full and bright.

5 O happy, happy that I am!
If thou canst be, O Faith,
The treasure that thou art in life,
What wilt thou be in death!

1 LET me no more my comfort draw
From my frail hold of Thee:
In this alone rejoice with awe,—
Thy mighty grasp of me.

2 Out of that weak, unquiet drift
That comes but to depart,
To that pure Heaven my spirit lift
Where Thou unchanging art.

3 Thy purpose of eternal good
Let me but surely know,
On this I'll lean, let changing mood
And feeling come or go;

4 Glad when Thy sunshine fills my soul,
Not lorn when clouds o'ercast;
Since Thou within Thy sure control
Of love dost hold me fast.

JAMES CAMPBELL SHAIRP, 1888. Abr.

Faith.

163 **God moves in a mysterious way.**

C. M.   *"We know that all things work together for good to them that love God."*   **Abdiel.**

WILLIAM COWPER, 1772.   M. WOOLSEY STRYKER, 1882.

1. GOD moves in a mysterious way, His wonders to perform; He plants His footsteps in the sea, And rides upon the storm.

2 Deep in unfathomable mines
  Of never-failing skill,
  He treasures up His bright designs,
  And works His sovereign will.

3 Ye fearful saints, new courage take;
  The clouds, ye so much dread,
  Are big with mercy, and shall break
  In blessings on your head!

4 His purposes will ripen fast,
  Unfolding every hour;

The bud may have a bitter taste,
  But sweet will be the flower.

5 Judge not the Lord by feeble sense,
  But trust Him for His grace;
  Behind a frowning providence,
  He hides a smiling face.

6 Blind unbelief is sure to err,
  And scan His work in vain:
  God is His own interpreter,
  And He will make it plain.

164 **Thro Baca's vale my way is cast.**

C. M.   *"Blessed is the man in whose heart are the highways."*   **London.**

SAMUEL D. ROBBINS, 1869.   ANDRO HART'S SCOTCH PSALTER 1635.
    Alt. in JOHN PLAYFORD'S PSALTER, 1671.

1. THRO Baca's vale my way is cast, Its thorns my feet have trod; But I have found the well at last, And quench my thirst in God!

2 My roof is but an humble home
  Hid in the wilderness:
  But o'er me springs th' eternal dome;
  For He my dwelling is.

3 My raiment rude and lowly seems,
  All travel-stained and old:
  But with His brightest morning beams
  He doth my soul infold.

Faith.

4 My table scantily is spread,
   With tears my cup o'erflows :
   But He is still my daily bread,
   No want my spirit knows.

5 Hard is the stony-pillowed bed,
   How broken is my rest!
   On Him I lean my aching head,
   And sleep upon His breast.

6 For faith can make the desert bloom,
   And thro the vistas dim,
   Love sees, in sunlight or in gloom,
   All pathways lead to Him.

165

1 My heart is resting, O my God,
   I will give thanks and sing;
   My heart is at the secret source
   Of every precious thing.

2 I thirst for springs of heavenly life,
   And here all day they rise;
   I seek the treasure of Thy love,
   And close at hand it lies.

3 And a new song is in my mouth
   To long-loved music set,
   Glory to Thee for all the grace
   I have not tasted yet.

4 I have a heritage of joy
   That yet I must not see,
   The hand that bled to make it mine
   Is keeping it for me.

5 'Thou art my portion, O my God!'
   Ten thousand voices say,
   The cadence of their glad *Amen*
   Will never die away.
                              ANNA L. WARING, 1854. *Abr.*

166   Tho lowly here our lot may be.

C. M.   "*O man greatly beloved, fear not. Peace be unto thee. Be strong, yea, be strong.*" Exaltation.
WILLIAM GASKELL, 1837. *Abr.*   HUBERT P. MAIN, 1896.

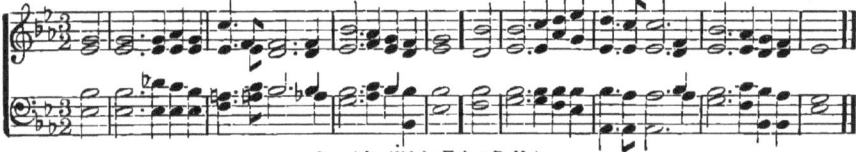

Copyright, 1896, by Hubert P. Main.

1 THO lowly here our lot may be,
   High work have we to do,
   In faith, O Lord, to follow Thee,
   Whose lot was lowly too.

2 Our days of darkness we may bear,
   Strong in our Father's love;
   We lean on His almighty arm,
   And fix our hopes above.

3 Our lives enriched with gentle thoughts
   And loving deeds may be,
   As streams, that still the nobler grow,
   The nearer to the sea.

4 To duty firm, to conscience true,
   However tried and prest,
   In God's clear sight high work we do,
   If we but do our best.

167 We bless Thee for Thy peace, O God!

C. M.   *"A kingdom that cannot be shaken."*   **Clark.**

ANON, 1862.   HUBERT P. MAIN, 1869.

1. WE bless Thee for Thy peace, O God!
Deep as the soundless sea,
Which falls like sunshine on the road
Of those who trust in Thee.

2 That peace which suffers and is strong,
Trusts where it cannot see,
Deems not the trial way too long,
But leaves the end with Thee.

3 That peace which flows serene and deep,
A river in the soul,
Whose banks a living verdure keep,
God's sunshine o'er the whole.

4 Such, Father! give our hearts such peace,
Whate'er the outward be,
Till all life's discipline shall cease,
And we go home to Thee.

168

1 O FOR a faith that will not shrink,
Tho pressed by many a foe,
That will not tremble on the brink
Of poverty or woe.

2 A faith that shines more bright and clear
When tempests rage without,
That when in danger knows no fear,
In darkness feels no doubt.

3 That will not murmur nor complain,
Beneath the chastening rod:
But in the hour of grief or pain
Can lean upon its God.

WILLIAM H. B. BATHURST, 1830. *Abr.*

169 The Lord's my Shepherd; I'll not want.

C. M.   *"For this God is our God forever and ever."*   **Arlington.**

FRANCIS ROUS, 1643.   THOMAS A. ARNE, 1762.

1. THE Lord's my Shepherd; I'll not want.
He makes me down to lie
In pastures green; He leadeth me
The quiet waters by.

Faith

2 My soul He doth restore again;
   And me to walk doth make
Within the paths of righteousness,
   Ev'n for His own name's sake.

3 Yes, tho I walk in death's dark vale,
   Yet will I fear no ill;
For Thou art with me, and Thy rod
   And staff me comfort still.

4 My table Thou hast furnished,
   In presence of my foes.
My head Thou dost with oil anoint,
   And my cup overflows.

5 Goodness and mercy, all my life,
   Shall surely follow me,
And in God's house forevermore
   My dwelling-place shall be.

170   To God I lift mine eyes.

6.6.6.6.8.8.   "Having therefore obtained the help that is from God, I stand unto this day."   **Lintz.**

Isaac Watts, 1719.   William B. Bradbury, 1857

Marcato.

1. To God I lift mine eyes; The God that built the skies, From Him is all mine aid, And Earth and na-ture made. God is the tower to which I fly, His grace is nigh in ev-ery hour.

2 My feet shall never slide,
   And fall in fatal snares;
Since God, my Guard and Guide,
   Defends me from my fears.
Those wakeful eyes which never sleep,
Shall Israel keep when dangers rise.

3 Since Thou hast pledged Thy word
   To save my soul from death,
Shall I not trust Thee, Lord,
   To keep my mortal breath!
I'll go and come, nor fear to die,
Till from on high Thou call me home.

Faith.

171 The Lord is my Shepherd.

11.11.11.11.11.   *"They know not the voice of a stranger."*   **Poland.**

James Montgomery, 1822. Abr.

Thomas Koschat, 1862.
Arr. Benjamin C. Blodgett, 1885.

1. The Lord is my Shepherd; no want shall I know. I feed in green pastures, safe fold-ed I rest. He leadeth my soul where the still wa-ters flow, Restores me when wand'ring, redeems when op-prest, Re-stores me when wand'ring, redeems when op-prest.

2 Thro valley and shadow of death tho I stray,
  Since Thou art my Guardian, no evil I fear;
  Thy rod shall defend me, Thy staff be my stay;
  No harm can befall me, my Comforter near.

3 Let goodness and mercy, my bountiful God,
  Still follow my steps till I meet Thee above;
  I seek, by the path which my forefathers trod,
  Thro lands of their sojourn, Thy kingdom of love.

Faith.

172 I mourn no more my vanished years.

C. M. *" In full age, like as a shock of corn cometh."* St. Frances.

JOHN G. WHITTIER, 1861. *Abr.* G. A. LÖHR, 1855.

1. I MOURN no more my van - ished years; Be - neath a ten - der rain,
2. The west - winds blow and sing - ing low I hear the glad streams run,

An A - pril rain, of smiles and tears, My heart is young a - gain.
The win - dows of my soul I throw Wide o - pen to the sun.

3 I break my pilgrim-staff, I lay
  Aside the toiling oar;
  The angel sought so far away
  I welcome at my door.

4 The woods shall wear their robes of
  The south-wind softly sigh,   [praise,
  And sweet, calm days in golden haze
  Melt down the amber sky.

5 All as God wills, who wisely heeds
  To give and to withhold,
  And knoweth more of all my needs
  Than all my prayers have told.

6 Enough that blessings undeserved
  Have marked mine erring track,
  That wheresoe'er my feet have swerved,
  His chastening turned me back,

7 That more and more a providence
  Of Love is understood,
  Making the springs of time and sense
  Sweet with eternal good,

8 That death seems but a covered way
  Which opens into light,
  Wherein no blinded child can stray
  Beyond the Father's sight!

9 That care and trial seem at last,
  Thro memory's sunset air,
  Like mountain ranges overpast,
  In purple distance fair.

10 And so the shadows fall apart,
  And so the west winds play,
  And all the windows of my heart
  I open to the day!

173 # My times are in Thy hand.

S. M.   *" I waited patiently for the Lord."*   **Adrian.**

WILLIAM F. LLOYD, 1835.   JOHN E. GOULD, 1846.

1. My times are in Thy hand; My God, I wish them there;
My life, my friends, my soul, I leave En-tire-ly to Thy care.

2 My times are in Thy hand,
   Whatever they may be;
Pleasing or painful, dark or bright,
   As best may seem to Thee.

3 My times are in Thy hand;
   Why should I doubt or fear?
A Father's hand will never cause
   His child a needless tear.

174 # Jesus, day by day.

5.5.8.8.5.5.   *" He that hath mercy on them shall lead them."*   **Hafodwen.**

NICOLAUS L. VON ZINZENDORF, 1721.   PETER MAURICE, 1876.
Tr. CATH. WINKWORTH, 1862.

1. Je-sus, day by day Guide us on life's way, Naught of dangers will we reck-on, Simply haste where

Faith.

Thou dost beckon, Lead us by the hand To our Fa-ther-land.

2 Hard should seem our lot,
    Let us waver not,
Never murmur at our crosses;
In dark days of grief and losses;
    'Tis thro trial we
    Here must pass to Thee.

3 When the heart must know
    Pain for other's woe,
When beneath its own, 'tis sinking,
Give us patience, hope unshrinking,
    Fix our eyes, O Friend,
    On our journey's end.

4 Thus our path shall be
    Daily traced by Thee;
Draw Thou nearer when 'tis rougher,
Help us most when most we suffer,
    And when all is o'er,
    Ope to us Thy door.

175   If thro unruffled seas.

S. M.   *" Our hearts shall rejoice in Him, because we have trusted in His holy name."*   **Monsell.**

Augustus M. Toplady, 1772. *Abr. Alt.*   Joseph Barnby, 1868.

1 If, thro unruffled seas,
    Toward Heaven we calmly sail,
With grateful hearts, O God, to Thee,
    We'll own the favoring gale.

2 Or should the surges rise
    And peace delay to come,
Blest is the sorrow, kind the storm,
    That drives us nearer home.

3 Soon shall our doubts and fears
    Subside at Thy control:
Thy loving-kindness shall break thro
    The midnight of the soul.

4 Teach us, in every state,
    To make Thy will our own;
And when the joys of sense depart,
    To live by faith alone ;—

5 Still on Thy plighted love
    At all events rely ;
The very hidings of Thy face
    Shall brighten by and by.

6 Blest is the man, O God,
    That stays himself on Thee !
Who waits for Thy salvation, Lord,
    Shall Thy salvation see.

176   Commit thou all thy griefs.

S. M.   "I AM THAT I AM."   **Peace.**

Ger. Paul Gerhardt, 1659.
Tr. John Wesley, 1739. *Abr.*

Alexander E. Fesca, 1849.

1. COM - MIT thou all thy griefs And ways in - to His hands,....

To His sure truth and ten - der care, Who Earth and Heav'n com - mands.

2 Who points the clouds their course,
  Whom wind and seas obey,
He shall direct thy wandering feet,
  He shall prepare thy way.

3 Thou on the Lord rely,
  So safe shalt thou go on.
Fix on His work thy steadfast eye,
  So shall thy work be done.

4 No profit canst thou gain
  By self-consuming care:
To Him commend thy cause; His ear
  Attends the softest prayer.

5 Give to the winds thy fears,
  Hope, and be undismayed;
God hears thy sighs and counts thy tears,
  God shall lift up thy head.

6 Thro waves and clouds and storms
  He gently clears thy way;
Wait thou His time, so shall this night
  Soon end in joyous day.

7 Far, far above thy thought
  His counsel shall appear,
When fully He the work hath wrought
  That caused thy needless fear.

8 THOU everywhere hast sway,
  And all things serve Thy might,
Thine every act pure blessing is,
  Thy path unsullied light.

9 Let us in life and death
  Thy sovereign truth declare,
And publish with our latest breath
  Thy love and guardian care!

Faith.

177   Lord, Thou art my Rock of strength.

7, D.   *"I am the Lord that healeth thee."*   **Blumenthal.**

Ger. AUGUST HERMANN FRANKE. 1711.   JACQUES BLUMENTHAL, 1849.
Tr. CATHERINE WINKWORTH, 1855. *Abr.*   *Har. by* HUBERT P. MAIN, 1883.

1. LORD, Thou art my Rock of strength, And my home is in Thine arms; Thou wilt send me

help at length, I can feel no wild a-larms. Sin nor death can pierce that shield

Thy de-fence has o'er me thrown; Unto Thee my-self I yield,—All my sor-rows are Thine own.

Arr. Copyright, 1883, by Hubert P. Main.

2 Let Thy mercy's wings be spread
O'er me, keep me close to Thee;
In the peace Thy love doth shed
Let me dwell eternally.
Be mine all! In all I do
Let me only seek Thy will;—
When my heart to Thee is true,
All is peaceful, calm and still.

178

1 CAST thy burden on the Lord,
Only lean upon His word;
Thou wilt soon have cause to bless
His eternal faithfulness.
Human counsels come to naught;
That shall stand which God hath wrought;
His compassion, love, and power
Are the same for evermore.

ANON, 1783. *Abr,*

Hope.

179 Head of the Church triumphant.

"Till Thy people pass over, O Lord, till the people pass over which Thou hast purchased."

7.7.8.7, D.
CHARLES WESLEY, 1745. Abr.

Septuor.
Arr. from LUDWIG VAN BEETHOVEN, 1799.

Alla marcia.

1. HEAD of the Church tri-umph-ant, We joy-ful-ly a-dore Thee! Till Thou ap-pear Thy members here Shall sing like those in glo-ry. We lift our hearts and voic-es With blest an-tic-i-pa-tion, And cry aloud, and give to God The praise of our sal-va-tion.

2 Thou dost conduct Thy people
Thro torrents of temptation;
Nor will we fear,
While Thou art near,
The fire of tribulation.
We clap our hands exulting
In Thine almighty favor;
Thy love divine
That makes us Thine,
Shall keep us Thine forever!

3 By faith we see the glory
To which Thou shalt restore us,
The world despise
For that high prize
Which Thou hast set before us;
And if Thou count us worthy,
We each, as dying Stephen,
Shall see Thee stand
At God's right hand
To take us up to Heaven!

Hope.

180   **Fear not, O ye little flock.**

7s, D.   *"The Lord shall be for strength to them that turn the battle to the gate."*   **Prussian Hymn.**

GUSTAVUS ADOLPHUS, 1631.
Based upon tr. of CATH. WINKWORTH, 1855.

PRUSSIAN AIR.

1. FEAR not, O ye lit - tle flock! Meet the foe-man's fiercest shock, While they press on

ev-ery side, In Al-might-y God con-fide. Tho your cour-age some-times faints, He will

tri-umph for His saints; All that now de - rides His power Last - eth on - ly one brief hour.

Copyright.

2 Take good cheer! The cause belongs
Unto God, to right your wrongs.
Dread ye not tho ills impend;
He will give a glorious end.
Hidden yet from mortal eyes,
His salvation shall arise.
Lo! He girdeth on His sword;
Trust the battle to your Lord.

3 Sure our hope as Christ is true,
Hate shall but itself undo,
Hell's array be overthrown;
GOD WITH US! we are His own.
Now, Lord Jesus, grant our prayer,
Make Thine arm of victory bare;
So shall saints and martyrs raise
One great anthem to Thy praise.

181   My soul, be on thy guard.

S. M.   *"Let not thine hands be slack."*   **Aswarby.**

George Heath, 1781.   Samuel Wesley, 1798

1 My soul, be on thy guard;
  Ten thousand foes arise,
And hosts of sin are pressing hard
  To draw thee from the skies.

2 Oh watch, and fight, and pray,
  The battle ne'er give o'er:
Renew it boldly every day,
  And help divine implore. ·

3 Ne'er think the victory won,
  Nor once at ease sit down;
Thine arduous work will not be done
  Till thou receive thy crown.

4 Fight on, my soul, till death
  Shall bring thee to thy God.
He'll take thee, at thy parting breath,
  To His divine abode.

182   Come, we that love the Lord.

S. M.   *"The Lord is on my side."*   **Laban.**

Isaac Watts, 1707. *Abr.*   Lowell Mason, 1830.

1. Come, we that love the Lord, And let our joys be known; Join in a song, with sweet ac - cord, And thus surround His throne.

2 The hill of Zion yields
  A thousand sacred sweets;
Before we reach the heavenly fields,
  Or walk the golden streets.

3 Then let our songs abound,
  And every tear be dry;
We're marching thro Immanuel's ground,
  To fairer worlds on high.

183 My soul, weigh not thy life.

S. M.   *" I will sing unto the Lord ; for He hath triumphed gloriously."*   **Ferguson.**

LEONARD SWAIN, 1858.   GEORGE KINGSLEY, 1843.

1. My soul, weigh not thy life A - gainst thy heav'n - ly crown,

Nor suf - fer Sa - tan's dead - liest strife To beat thy cour - age down.

2 The battle soon will yield,
   If thou thy part fulfil ;
For strong as is the hostile shield,
Thy sword is stronger still.

3 Thine armor is divine
   Thy feet with victory shod,
And on thy head shall quickly shine
The diadem of God.

184 O Saviour, I have naught to plead.

8.8.8.6.   *" I have seen God face to face and my life is preserved."*   **Esthwaite.**

JANE FOX CREWDSON, 1864.   H. BARRY.

1 O SAVIOUR, I have naught to plead,
   In Earth beneath or Heaven above,
But just mine own exceeding need
   And Thine exceeding love.

2 The need will soon be past and gone,
   Exceeding great but quickly o'er :
The love unbought is all Thine own
   And lasts for evermore.

185   Leave God to order all thy ways.

"Blessed are they that mourn, for they shall be comforted."

8.8.8.8.8.8.

Ger. GEORGE NEUMARK, 1653.
Tr. CATH. WINKWORTH, 1855. *Abr.*

"Wer nur den lieben Gott lässt walten."

GEORGE NEUMARCK, 1657.
Har. JOHANN SEB. BACH, d. 1750.

1. { Leave God to or-der all thy ways, And hope in Him what-e'er be-tide;
Thou'lt find Him, in the e-vil days, Thine all-suf-fi-cient strength and guide. }

Who trusts in God's un-chang-ing love Builds on the Rock that naught can move!

2 Only thy restless heart keep still,
    And wait in cheerful hope, content
To take whate'er His gracious will,
    His all-discerning love hath sent.
Doubt not our inmost wants are known
To Him who chose us for His own.

3 Sing, pray, and swerve not from His ways:
    But do thine own part faithfully.
Trust His rich promises of grace,
    So shall they be fulfilled in thee;
God never yet forsook at need
The soul that trusted Him indeed.

186

1 SURROUNDED by unnumbered foes,
    Against my soul the battle goes:

Yet tho I weary, sore distrest,
    I know that I shall reach my rest;
I lift my tearful eyes above,—
    His banner over me is love!

2 Its sword my spirit will not yield,
    Tho flesh may faint upon the field;
He waves before my fading sight
The branch of palm, the crown of light;
I lift my brightening eyes above,—
    His banner over me is love!

3 My cloud of battle-dust may dim,
    His veil of splendor curtain, Him,
And in the midnight of my fear
    I may not feel Him standing near:
But, as I lift mine eyes above,
    His banner over me is love!

GERALD MASSEY, 1869.

Hope.

187   Christian, dost thou see them!

6s & 5s, D.   *" We wrestle not with flesh and blood."*   **St. Andrews.**

Gk. ANDREW OF CRETE, *cir.* 720   JOHN B. DYKES, 1868.
Tr. JOHN M. NEALE, 1862.

1. CHRIS-TIAN, dost thou see them! On the ho - ly ground, How the troops of dark - ness Prowl thy steps a - round? Chris-tian, up and smite them! Count-ing gain but loss, Smite them by the mer - it Of the ho - ly Cross.

2 Christian! dost thou feel them,
How they work within,
Striving, tempting, luring,
Goading on to sin?
Christian, never tremble!
Never yield to fear;
Smite them by the virtue
Of unceasing prayer.

3 Christian! dost thou hear them,
How they speak thee fair?
"Always fast and vigil?
Always watch and prayer?"
Christian! answer boldly,—
"While I breathe I pray!"
Peace shall follow battle,
Night shall end in day.

4 "Well I know thy trouble,
O My servant true!
Thou art very weary,—
I was weary too:
But that toil shall make thee
Some day all Mine own;
And the end of sorrow
Shall be near My throne."

188 Since o'er Thy footstool here.

6.6.6.6.8.8.   *" His children shall have a place of refuge."*   **Holyoke.**

William A. Muhlenberg, 1874. *Alt.*   Benjamin C. Blodgett, 1884.

1. Since o'er Thy foot - stool here, Great God, such gems are strewn, Oh, what mag -
nif - i - cence Must glow a - bout Thy throne! So brilliant these but
drops of light— There o - cean tides roll deep and bright.

So bril - liant
There o - - cean

Copyright, 1885, by Biglow & Main.

2 If night's blue-curtained sky,
   With constellations wrought,
Like royal canopy,
   With matchless diamonds fraught,
Be, Lord, Thy temple's outer vail,
What splendors at the shrine must dwell!

3 Can these dim eyes endure
   That noon of living rays!
These spirits so impure
   Upon Thy brightness gaze!
In mercy, Lord, anoint our sight,
And robe us for that world of light!

189 Long did I toil, and knew no earthly rest.

10.10.10.10.10.10.   *"My Beloved is mine, and I am His."*   **Evensong.**

HENRY F. LYTE, 1833. *Abr.*   WALTER BOND GILBERT, 1873.

Andante.

1. LONG did I toil, and knew no earth-ly rest, Far did I rove and found no cer-tain home;
2. The good I have is from His stores supplied,Tho ill is on - ly what He deems the best.

At last I sought them in His shelt'ring breast,Who opes His arms and bids the wea-ry come!
He for my Friend,—I'm rich with nought beside,And poor with-out Him, tho of all pos - sest.

With Him I found a home, a rest di - vine, And I since then am His and He is mine.
Changes may come,—I take, or I re - sign, Con-tent, while I am His while He is mine!

By permission.

3 While here, alas! I know but half His love,
　But half discern Him, and but half adore:
　But when I meet Him in the realms above,
　I hope to love Him better, praise Him more,
　And feel and tell, amid the choir divine,
　How fully I am His and He is mine!

Love.

190   Strong Son of God, Immortal Love.

"The Creation itself also shall be delivered from the bondage of corruption, into the liberty of the glory of the children of God."

L. M.

ALFRED TENNYSON, 1849.

Alsace.

LUDWIG VAN BEETHOVEN, 1800. *Arr.*

1. STRONG Son of God, Im - mor - tal love, Whom we, that have not seen Thy face,
By faith, and faith a - lone, em - brace, Be - liev - ing where we can - not prove:

2 Thine are these orbs of light and shade,
Thou madest life in man and brute,
Thou madest Death, and lo, Thy foot
Is on the skull which Thou hast made!

3 Thou seemest human and divine,
The highest, holiest manhood, Thou:
Our wills are ours, we know not how;
Our wills are ours, to make them Thine.

4 Our little systems have their day,
They have their day and cease to be;
They are but broken lights of Thee,
And Thou, O Lord, art more than they.

5 That God, which ever lives and loves,—
One God, one law, one element,
And one far-off divine event,
To which the whole Creation moves.

191

1 O LOVE of God, how strong and true!
Eternal and yet ever new,
Uncomprehended and unbought,
Beyond all knowledge and all thought!

2 O heavenly Love, how precious still
In days of weariness and ill,
In nights of pain and helplessness,
To heal, to comfort, and to bless!

3 We read thee best in Him who came
To bear for us the cross of shame,
Sent by the Father from on high,
Our life to live our death to die.

4 O Love of God, our shield and stay
Thro all the perils of our way,
Eternal Love, in Thee we rest,
Forever safe, forever blest!

HORATIUS BONAR. *Abr.*

192 Jesus! and shall it ever be.

"Take heed lest there shall be any one that maketh spoil of you thro his philosophy!"

L. M.
JOSEPH GRIGG, 1730?
Alt. BENJAMIN FRANCIS, 1787.

Federal Street.
HENRY K. OLIVER, 1832.

1 JESUS, and shall it ever be,
A mortal man ashamed of Thee?
Ashamed of Thee, whom angels praise,
Whose glories shine thro endless days?

2 Ashamed of Jesus! sooner far
Let evening blush to own her star;
He sheds the beams of light divine,
O'er this benighted soul of mine.

3 Ashamed of Jesus! just as soon
Let midnight be ashamed of noon;
'Twas midnight with my soul, till He,
Bright morning star, bid darkness flee.

4 Ashamed of Jesus! that dear friend,
On whom my hopes of heaven depend!
No; when I blush, be this my shame,
That I no more revere His name.

5 Ashamed of Jesus! yes, I may,
When I've no guilt to wash away,
No tear to wipe, no good to crave,
No fears to quell, no soul to save.

6 Till then, nor is my boasting vain!
Till then I boast a Saviour slain.
And oh, may this my glory be,
That Christ is not ashamed of me!

193 Faithful, O Lord, Thy mercies are.

C. M.
" Until the times of restoration of all things."
CHARLES WESLEY, 1762. Abr.

Lancaster.
SAMUEL HOWARD, 1762.

1. FAITHFUL, O Lord, Thy mercies are, A rock that cannot move; A thousand prom-is-es declare Thy constancy of love.

2 Its streams the whole Creation reach,
So plenteous is the store;
Enough for all, enough for each,
Enough for evermore.

3 Thro all the universe it reigns,
Unalterably sure;
And while Thy truth O God remains
Thy goodness must endure.

194 We love Thee, Lord, yet not alone.

C. M.   " *A little while, and ye shall see Me.*"   St. Mark.

JULIA A. ELLIOTT. *Abr.*   HENRY J. GAUNTLETT, 1872

1. WE love Thee, Lord, yet not a - lone, Be - cause Thy boun-teous hand

Showers down its rich and cease - less gifts On o - cean and on land;

195

2 'Tis not alone because Thy names
Of wisdom, power, and love,
Are written on the Earth beneath,
The glorious skies above;

3 We love Thee, Lord, because when we
Had erred and gone astray,
Thou didst recall our wandering souls
Into the heavenward way.

4 Because, when we forsook Thy ways,
Nor kept Thy holy will,
Thou wast not the avenging Judge,
But gracious Father still.

5 Because, when we were bound by sin,
Thou gavest hopes of Heaven;
Yes; much we love,who much have sinned,
And much have been forgiven!

1 IT was no love of mine, dear Lord,
That won Thy love to me;
On me were Thy compassions poured
From that accursèd Tree.

2 And now I hold Thee by no bands
Of saintly prayer or deed:
I hold Thee with my trembling hands,
These hands of guilt and need.

3 Saviour and sinner we have met,
And meeting will not part;
The blood that bought me claims me yet,—
Christ hath me in His heart!

4 So, poor yet rich and vile yet pure,
I have mine all in Thee,
Beloved and loving, pledged, secure,
To all Eternity.

HERVEY D. GANSE, 1887.

196 Thou Grace Divine, encircling all.

C. M. *"They also shall overcome that are with Him, called, and chosen, and faithful."* **Albano.**

ELIZA SCUDDER, 1852. VINCENT NOVELLO, 1861.

1. Thou Grace Di - vine, en - cir - cling all, A shore - less sound - less sea,

Where - in at last our souls must fall, O Love of God most free!

2 When over dizzy heights we go,
   One soft hand blinds our eyes,
   The other leads us safe and slow,
   O Love of God most wise!

3 And tho we turn us from Thy face,
   And wander wide and long,
   Thou holdest still in Thine embrace,
   O Love of God most strong'

4 The saddened heart, the restless soul,
   The toil-worn frame and mind,
   Alike confess Thy sweet control,
   O Love of God most kind!

5 And, filled and quickened by Thy breath,
   Our souls are strong and free
   To rise o'er sin and fear and death,
   O Love of God, to Thee.

197

1 O LORD! I would delight in Thee,
   And on Thy care depend;
   To Thee in every trouble flee,
   My best, my only Friend.

2 When all created streams are dried,
   Thy fullness is the same;
   May I with this be satisfied,
   And glory in Thy name!

3 Why should the soul a drop bemoan,
   Who has a fountain near,
   A fountain which will ever run
   With waters sweet and clear?

4 No good in creatures can be found,
   But may be found in Thee;
   I must have all things and abound,
   While God is God to me!

JOHN RYLAND, 1777 *Abr.*

Love.

198   When this passing world is done.

7.7.7.7.7.7.   *"He changed his prison garments."*   **Margaret Street.**

ROBERT MURRAY MCCHEYNE, 1837. *Abr.*   ALEXANDER S. COOPER, 1872.

1. WHEN this passing world is done, When has sunk yon glorious Sun, When I stand with Christ in light,

All my finished life in sight; Then, Lord, shall I ful-ly know, Not till then, how much I owe.

2 When I stand before the throne,
Clothed in beauty not my own,
When I see Thee as Thou art,
Love Thee with unsinning heart,
Then, Lord, shall I fully know,
Not till then, how much I owe!

3 When the praise of Heaven I hear,
Loud as thunders to the ear,
Loud as many waters' noise,
Sweet as harps' melodious voice,
Then, Lord, shall I fully know,
Not till then, how much I owe!

199   God, my King, Thy might confessing.

8s & 7s.   *"Thy condescension hath made me great."*   **Trust.**

RICHARD MANT, 1832. *Abr.*   FELIX MENDELSSOHN BARTHOLDY, 1840. *Alt.*

1. GOD, my King, Thy might con - fess - ing, Ev - er will I bless Thy name;

Love.

Day by day Thy throne ad-dress-ing, Still will I Thy praise pro-claim.

2 Age to age shall teach Thy glory,
On Thy might and greatness dwell,
Speak of Thy dread acts the story,
And Thy deeds of wonder tell.

3 Full of kindness and compassion,
Slow to anger, vast in love,
God is good to all creation;
All His works His goodness prove.

200 Jesus, engrave it on my heart.

L. M.

" Thou wilt show me the path of life."

Zithri.

SAMUEL MEDLEY, 1789. *Abr.*

JOHANN STAHL, 1544.

Supplicando.

1. Je-sus, en-grave it on my heart That Thou the one thing need-ful art. I could from all things

part-ed be; But nev-er, nev-er, Lord, from Thee. A-men, A-men, A-men, A-men.

2 Needful Thy presence, dearest Lord,
True peace and comfort to afford.
Needful Thy promise, to impart
New life and vigor to my heart.

3 Needful art Thou, my Guide, my Stay,
Thro all life's dark and weary way;
Nor less in death Thou'lt needful be
To bring my spirit home to Thee. *Amen.*

201 Should I not, in meek adoring.

" We know and have believed the love which God hath."

8s & 7s, P.
Ger. Paul Gerhardt, 1656. Abr.
Tr. M. W. S., 1882.

"Sollt' ich meinem Gott nicht singen."

G. G. Bolze, 1788

1. Should I not, in meek a - dor - ing, Thank my gracious God a - bove, Whom I see on all things pour-ing Forth the sunshine of His love? For 'tis naught but Love's own lov - ing In His constant heart, doth care Endless - ly to love and bear Those their love, in ser - vice, proving. All things last their portioned day—God's love to e - ter - ni - ty.

rit.

2 O'er her young the eagle hovers,
  Spreading wide her wings' defence;
So, each day, my soul God covers
  Under His omnipotence.
Out of naught began my living,
  When the mighty Father bade,
  And the life that then He made
Still has shared His changeless giving.
  All things last their portioned day—
  God's love to eternity.

3 All-compassionate, the Father,
  For us gave His dear Firstborn,
In that Life-gift aye to gather
  Home the orphaned and forlorn.
O Thou vast immeasured Kindness!
  Deep unfathomable Sea!
  Who can bound Thy mystery?
Human wisdom owns her blindness.
  All things last their portioned day—
  God's love to eternity.

202 Come, O Thou Traveller unknown.

8.8.8.8.8.8.   *"I have seen God face to face and my life is preserved."*   **Melita.**
CHARLES WESLEY, 1742. *Abr.*   JOHN B. DYKES, 1861.

1. COME, O Thou Tra-vel - ler un-known,Whom still I hold, but cannot see. My com - pa-ny be - fore is gone,

And I am left a - lone with Thee; Wrestling, I will not let Thee go, Till I Thy Name,Thy nature know.

203

2 I need not tell Thee who *I* am;
My misery or sin declare.
Thyself hast call'd me by my name.—
Look on Thy hands, and read it there!
But who, I ask Thee, who art Thou?
Tell me Thy Name, and tell me now.

3 'Tis Love! 'tis Love! Thou diedst for me!
I hear Thy whisper in my heart!
The morning breaks, the shadows flee!
Pure universal Love Thou art!
In vain I have not wept and strove;
Thy Nature, and Thy Name, is Love!

4 Lame as I am, I take the prey!
Hell, earth, and sin with ease o'ercome.
I leap for joy, pursue my way,
And as a bounding hart fly home,
Thro all eternity to prove
Thy Nature and Thy Name is Love.

1 THOU art, O God, the life and light
Of all this wondrous world we see;
Its glow by day, its smile by night,
Are but reflections caught from Thee.
Where'er we turn Thy glories shine,
And all things fair and bright are Thine.

2 When day, with farewell beam, delays
Among the opening clouds of even,
And we can almost think we gaze
Thro golden vistas into Heaven,
Those hues that make the Sun's decline
So soft, so radiant, Lord, are Thine.

3 When youthful spring around us breathes,
Thy spirit warms her fragrant sigh;
And every flower the summer wreathes
Is born beneath that kindling eye.
Where'er we turn, Thy glories shine,
And all things fair and bright are Thine.

THOMAS MOORE, 1816. *Abr.*

204 We cannot always trace the way.

8.8.8.4. " On whatsoever errand I shall send thee, thou shalt go." **Woodthorpe.**

JOHN BOWRING, 1824. JAMES ADCOCK, d. 1860.

Andante.

1. WE can-not al-ways trace the way Where Thou, our gracious Lord, dost move: But we can al-ways

sure - ly say That Thou art Love.

2 When fear its gloomy cloud will fling
O'er Earth, our souls to Heav'n above,
As to their sanctuary spring;
For Thou art Love.

3 When mystery shrouds our darkened path,
We'll check our dread, our doubts reprove;
In this our soul sweet comfort hath,
That Thou art Love.

205 Blessèd are the pure in heart.

7.7.7.7. " Earnestly desiring the coming of the day of God." **University College.**

JOHN M. NEALE, 1844. HENRY J. GAUNTLETT, 1848.

1. BLESSED are the pure in heart!
They have loved the better part.
When life's journey they have trod,
They shall go to see their God.

2 Till in glory they appear,
They shall often see Him here;
And His grace shall learn to know,
In His glorious works below.

3 When the Sun begins to rise,
Spreading brightness thro the skies,
They will love to praise and bless
Christ, the Sun of Righteousness.

4 In the watches of the night,
When the stars are clear and bright,
'Thus the just shall shine,' they say,
'In the resurrection day.'

5 God in everything they see.
First in all their thoughts is He.
They have loved the better part,—
Blessèd are the pure in heart.

206   When glorious in the nightly sky.

C. M.   *"The promise is to you and to your children."*   **Nottingham.**

HENRY F. LYTE, 1834. *Abr.*   HENRY J. GAUNTLETT, 1846.

1. WHEN glo - rious in the night - ly sky Thy moon and stars I see,

Oh, what is man! I won - d'ring cry, To be so loved by Thee!

2 To him Thou hourly deign'st to give
New mercies from on high;
Didst quit Thy Throne with him to live,
For him in pain to die.

3 Close to Thine own bright seraphim
His favored path is trod;
And all beside are serving him,
That he may serve his God.

207   There is no sorrow, Lord, too slight.

C. M.   *"Jesus wept."*   **St. Columba.**

JANE FOX CREWDSON, 1864. *Abr.*   ANCIENT IRISH TUNE. *Har.* ROBERT P. STEWART, 1874.

1. THERE is no sor-row, Lord, too slight, To bring in prayer to Thee; There is no burd'ning care too light To wake Thy sym-pa-thy.

2 There is no secret sigh we breathe
But meets Thine ear divine;
And every cross grows light beneath
The shadow, Lord, of Thine.

3 Life's ills without, sin's strife within,—
The heart would overflow,
But for that Love which died for sin,
That Love which wept with woe!

208 More love to Thee, O Christ!

6.4.6.4.6.6.4.   *" It is the voice of my Beloved that knocketh, saying ' Open to me.' "*   **Horbury.**

ELIZABETH PRENTISS, 1856. Abr.   JOHN B. DYKES, 1860.

Adagio.

1. More love to Thee, O Christ! More love to Thee! Hear Thou the prayer I make, On bend-ed knee;

This is my earn - est plea,—More love, O Christ! to Thee, More love to Thee!

2 Once earthly joy I craved,
Sought peace and rest
Now Thee alone I seek,
Give what is best.
This all my prayer shall be,—
More love, O Christ! to Thee,
More love to Thee!

3 Let sorrow do its work,
Send grief and pain;
Sweet are Thy messengers,
Sweet their refrain,
When they can sing with me,—
More love, O Christ, to Thee,
More love to Thee!

209 Nearer, my God, to Thee.

6.4.6.4,6.6.4.   *"Then shalt thou delight thyself in the Almighty, and shalt lift up thy face unto God."*   **Kedron.**

SARAH F. ADAMS, 1840.   A. B. SPRATT.

mf

1. Near-er, my God, to Thee, Near-er to Thee, E'en tho it be a cross, That rais-eth me;

Ped.

Love.

Still all my song shall be, Near-er, my God, to Thee, Near-er to Thee.

2 Tho like the wanderer,
  The Sun gone down,
Darkness be over me,
  My rest a stone;
Yet in my dreams I'd be
Nearer, my God, to Thee,
  Nearer to Thee!

3 There let the way appear
  Steps unto Heaven;
All that Thou sendest me
  In mercy given;
Angels to beckon me
Nearer, my God, to Thee,
  Nearer to Thee!

4 Then, with my waking thoughts
  Bright with Thy praise,
Out of my stony griefs
  Beth-El I'll raise;
So by my woes to be
Nearer, my God, to Thee,
  Nearer to Thee!

5 Or if, on joyful wing,
  Cleaving the sky,
Sun, moon, and stars forgot,
  Upward I fly,
Still, all my song shall be,
Nearer, my God, to Thee,
  Nearer to Thee!

6.4.6.4.6.6.6.4.   SECOND TUNE.   Bethany.
Lowell Mason, 1856.

210   O Christ, our true and only Light!

L. M.   *"The effect of righteousness shall be quietness and assurance."*   **Lebenslicht.**

Ger. JOHANN HERRMANN, 1630.
Tr. CATH. WINKWORTH, 1862. *Abr.*

JOSEPH CLAUDER'S "PSALMODIA," 1630.

1. O Christ, our true and on - ly Light! Il - lu-mine those who sit in night. Let those a - far now

JOHANN SCHOP, 1641. *Abr.*

hear Thy voice, And in Thy fold with us re - joice. A - men, A - men, A - men, A - men.

2 Fill with the radiance of Thy grace
The souls now lost in error's maze,
And all whom in their secret minds
Some dark delusion hurts and blinds.

3 Oh, make the deaf to hear Thy word,
And teach the dumb to speak, dear Lord,
Who dare not yet the faith avow,
Tho secretly they hold it now. *Amen.*

211   When at Thy footstool, Lord! I bend.

L. M.   *"Draw nigh to God, and He will draw nigh to you."*   **San Salvador.**

HENRY FRANCIS LYTE, 1833. *Abr.*

EMILIO PIERACCINI, 1848.

1. When at Thy foot - stool, Lord! I bend, And plead with Thee for mer - cy there.

Prayer.

Oh! think Thou of the sin - ner's Friend, And for His sake re - ceive my prayer.

212

2 Think, Lord! how I am still Thine own,
The trembling creature of Thy hand!
Think how my heart to sin is prone,
And what temptations round me stand.

3 Thine eye, Thine ear, they are not dull,
Thine arm can never shortened be;
Behold me here! my heart is full;
Behold and spare and succor me!

1 LORD! take my heart, and let it be
Forever closed to all but Thee.
Seal Thou my breast, and let me wear
That pledge of love forever there.

2 How blest are they, who still abide
Close sheltered in Thy bleeding side!
Who thence their life and strength derive,
And by Thee move and in Thee live.

Ger. NICOLAUS L. VON ZINZENDORF, 1735.
Tr. JOHN WESLEY, 1739. Abr.

213 Beneath all form and rite and creed.

L. M. *"That which is in part shall be done away."* **Retreat.**

M. W. S., 1889. *Abr* THOMAS HASTINGS, 1840.

1 BENEATH all form and rite and creed,
Behind all hymn and litany,
Beyond all outward word or deed,
My heart makes search, O Lord, for Thee.

2 Unreal to my weary mind
Thy very truths and sacraments,
Unless in these Thyself I find,
And find in Thee their inner sense.

3 O Son of God and Son of Man,
Thou knowest what I can not say!

I hold Thee fast as best I can;
Thrust not my feeble faith away.

4 Forgive me that I can not speak
What once I thought so well I knew!
I only know my flesh is weak,—
I only know that Thou art true.

5 Come nearer, Lord! Beside me stand.
Help me to praise where late I grieved.
Bring me to Thine unshadowed land,
With them who saw not, yet believed!

214   Out of the depths I cry to Thee.

" I hope shortly to see thee, and we shall speak face to face."

8.7.8.7.8.8.7.   **"Aus tiefer Noth."**

Ger. MARTIN LUTHER, 1524.   MARTIN LUTHER, 1524. *Har.*
Tr. CATH. WINKWORTH, 1858. *Abr.*

1. { Out of the depths I cry to Thee, Lord, hear me I im - plore Thee. }
  { Bend down Thy gracious ear to me, Let my prayer come be - fore Thee. } If Thou re -

memb'rest each misdeed, If each should have its right - ful meed, Lord, who could stand be-fore Thee!

2 And tho it tarry till the night
  And round till morning waken,
My heart shall ne'er misdoubt His might,
  Nor count itself forsaken;
Our God is merciful and just,
Here is my comfort and my trust,
  His help I wait unshaken.

215   Come, my soul! thy suit prepare.

7.7.7.7.   *" This is the boldness which we have toward Him."*   **Seymour.**

JOHN NEWTON, 1779. *Abr.*   CARL MARIA VON WEBER, 1826.
                ARR. BY TIMOTHY B. MASON, 1834.

1. Come, my soul! thy suit pre - pare; Je - sus loves to an - swer prayer.

Prayer.

He Him - self has bid thee pray, There - fore will not say thee nay.

2 Thou art coming to a King,
  Large petitions with thee bring;
  For His grace and power are such,
  None can ever ask too much.

3 Lord, I come to Thee for rest.
  Take possession of my breast.
  There Thy blood-bought right maintain,
  And without a rival reign.

4 As the image in the glass
  Answers the beholder's face,
  Thus unto my heart appear,
  Print Thine own resemblance there.

5 While I am a pilgrim here,
  Let Thy love my spirit cheer.
  Be my Guide, my Guard, my Friend,
  Lead me to my journey's end.

216   Father! whate'er of earthly bliss.

C. M.   "*Ask in faith, nothing doubting.*"   Dalehurst.

ANNE STEELE, 1760. *Abr.*   ARTHUR COTTMAN, 1872. *Har.* B. C. B.

1. FA - THER! what-e'er of earth - ly bliss Thy sovereign hand de - nies, Ac - cept-ed at Thy

throne of grace Let this pe - ti - tion rise.

2 Give me a calm, a thankful heart,
  From every murmur free.
  The blessings of Thy grace impart,
  And let me live to Thee.

3 Let the sweet hope, that Thou art mine,
  My path of life attend.
  Thy presence thro my journey shine,
  And bless its happy end.

217 Lead, kindly Light.

14.14.10.10. "*Blest'd be my Maker, who giveth me songs in the night.*" **Lux Benigna.**
JOHN HENRY NEWMAN, 1833. JOHN B. DYKES, 1865.

1. Lead, kindly Light, a - mid th'en-circling gloom, lead Thou me on; The night is dark, and I am far from home, lead Thou me on. Keep Thou my feet; I do not ask to see.... The dis - tant scene; one step e - nough for me. A - men.

2 I was not ever thus, nor prayed that Thou shouldst lead me on;
I loved to choose and see my path : but now—lead *Thou* me on!
I loved the garish day and, spite of fears,
Pride ruled my will :—remember not past years!

3 So long Thy power hath blest me, sure it still will lead me on,
O'er moor and fen, o'er crag and torrent, till the night is gone;
And, with the morn, those angel faces smile
Which I have loved long since, and lost awhile! *Amen.*

218   While Thee I seek, protecting Power.

C. M.   *" The prayers of the saints went up before God."*   **St. Flavian.**

HELEN MARIA WILLIAMS, 1786. *Abr.*   ABRAHAM BARBER'S PSALTER, 1687.

1 WHILE Thee I seek, protecting Power,
     Be my vain wishes stilled,
   And may this consecrated hour
     With better hopes be filled.

2 Thy love the powers of thought bestowed,
     To Thee my thoughts would soar;
   Thy mercy o'er my life has flowed,
     That mercy I adore.

3 In each event of life, how clear,
     Thy ruling hand I see!
   Each blessing to my soul more dear,
     Because conferred by Thee.

4 In every joy that crowns my days,
     In every pain I bear,
   My heart shall find delight in praise,
     Or seek relief in prayer.

219

1 I BOW my forehead in the dust,
     I veil mine eyes for shame,
   And urge, in trembling self-distrust,
     A prayer without a claim.

2 No offering of mine own I have,
     Nor works my faith to prove;
   I can but give the gifts He gave,
     And plead His love for love.

3 I know not where His islands lift
     Their fronded palms in air:
   I only know I cannot drift
     Beyond His love and care.

4 I know not what the future hath
     Of marvel or surprise,
   Assured alone that life or death
     His mercy underlies.

JOHN G. WHITTIER, 1867. *Abr.*

220

1 ALMIGHTY God, in humble prayer
     To Thee our souls we lift;
   Do Thou our waiting minds prepare
     For Thy most needful gift.

2 We ask not golden streams of wealth
     Along our path to flow;
   We ask not undecaying health,
     Nor length of years below.

3 We ask not honors which an hour
     May bring, or take away;
   We ask not pleasure, pomp, nor power,
     Lest we should go astray.

4 We ask for wisdom. Lord, impart
     The knowledge how to live,
   A wise and understanding heart
     To all before Thee give.

JAMES MONTGOMERY, 1825. *Abr.*

221 Guide me, O Thou great Jehovah.

8.7.8.7.4.7.
WILLIAM WILLIAMS, 1773.

" Continuing steadfastly in prayer."

Wildersmouth.
EDWARD J. HOPKINS, 1879.

1. GUIDE me, O Thou great Je - ho - vah! Pilgrim thro this barren laud. I am weak but Thou art

might-y; Hold me by Thy pow'rful hand. Bread of Heav - en, Feed me now and ev - er - more.

2 Open Thou the crystal fountain,
  Whence the healing streams do flow.
Let the fiery, cloudy pillar
  Lead me all my journey thro.
    Strong Deliverer,
  Be Thou still my Strength and Shield.

3 When I tread the verge of Jordan,
  Bid my anxious fear subside.
Death of death, and hell's Destruction,
  Land me safe on Canaan's side.
    Songs of praises
  I will ever give to Thee.

222 Call Jehovah thy salvation.

8.7.8.7.
JAMES MONTGOMERY, , 1822. *Abr.*

" He shall call upon Me, and I will answer him."

Nathanael.
HUBERT P. MAIN, 1880. *Abr.*

1. CALL Je - ho - vah thy sal - va - tion, Rest be - neath th'Al-might-y's shade. In His se - cret

Copyright, 1880, by Biglow & Main.

hab-it - a - tion Dwell, and nev-er be dismayed!

2 There no tumult can alarm thee,
  Thou shalt dread no hidden snare ;
Guile nor violence can harm thee,
  In eternal safeguard there.

3 Since with pure and firm affection,
  Thou on God hast set thy love,
With the wings of His protection
  He will shield thee from above.

223   Jesus! Lover of my soul!

7s, D.
CHARLES WESLEY, 1740. *Abr.*

"He maketh the storm a calm."

Treufest.
German, 1784.

Divoto.   FINE.

I. { Je - sus! Lov - er of my soul! Let me to Thy bo - som fly, }
{ While the near - er wa - ters roll, While the tem - pest still is high. }
D.C.—Safe in - to the ha - ven guide, Oh, re - ceive my soul at last.

D. C.

Hide me, O my Sav - iour, hide, Till the storm of life is past,

2 Other refuge have I none,
  Hangs my helpless soul on Thee;
Leave, ah! leave me not alone,
  Still support and comfort me!
All my trust on Thee is stayed,
  All my help from Thee I bring;
Cover my defenceless head,
  With the shadow of Thy wing.

3 Plenteous grace with Thee is found,
  Grace to cover all my sin;
Let the healing streams abound,
  Make and keep me pure within.
Thou of life the Fountain art;
  Freely let me take of Thee.
Spring Thou up within my heart,
  Rise to all eternity!

224 Love Divine, all loves excelling.

"That in the ages to come He might shew the exceeding riches of His grace in kindness toward us in Christ Jesus."

8s & 7s, D.   **Ecclesia.**

CHARLES WESLEY, 1746. *Abr.*   GERMAN, 1648.

1. { Love Di-vine, all loves ex-cel-ling, Joy of Heav'n, to Earth come down, }
{ Fix in us Thy humble dwelling, All Thy faith-ful mer-cies crown. } Je-sus, Thou art all compassion,

Pure unbounded love Thou art; Vis-it us with Thy sal-va-tion, En-ter ev-'ry trembling heart.

2 Breathe, oh, breathe, Thy loving Spirit
Into every troubled breast.
Let us all in Thee inherit.
Let us find Thy promised rest.
Come, almighty to deliver,
Let us all Thy life receive.
Suddenly return, and never,
Never more Thy temples leave.

3 Finish then Thy new creation,
Pure and spotless let us be.
Let us see our whole salvation
Perfectly secured by Thee.
Changed from glory into glory,
Till in Heaven we take our place,
Till we cast our crowns before Thee,
Lost in wonder, love and praise!

225 Come, ye disconsolate.

"To you it hath been granted in the behalf of Christ, not only to believe on Him : but also to suffer."

11.10.11.10.   **Come, ye disconsolate.**

THOMAS MOORE, 1816.   SAMUEL WEBBE, 1790. *Abr.*

1. Come, ye dis-con-so-late, wher-e'er ye languish. Come to the mer-cy-seat, fer-vent-ly kneel.
2. Joy of the des-o-late, Light of the straying, Hope of the pen-i-tent, fadeless and pure!

Here bring your wounded hearts, here tell your anguish; Earth has no sor-row that Heav'n cannot heal!
Here speaks the Com-fort-er, ten - der - ly say - ing, Earth has no sor-row that Heav'n cannot cure!

226   O God, forsake me not!

6.7.6.7.6.6.6.6.   **"Ach Gott verlass mich nicht."**

" That Thine hand might be with me."

Ger. SALOMON FRANCK, *d.* 1725. *Tr.* M. W. S., 1882.   1648. *Har.* JOHANN SEB. BACH, 1730.

Implorando.

1. { O God, for-sake me not! Thine hand to me ex-tend - ing, }
   { Un - til, in stead-y faith, My pil-grim - age is end - ing. } Here in this vale of night, Be

Thou my glo-rious light: Be Thou my staff and rod, Forsake me not, my God!..........

2 O God, forsake me not!
  Teach me Thy way to ponder,
  And let me nevermore
  In sin and folly wander.
  Give me the Holy Ghost
  Grant an all-conquering trust,
  And, if my footing slide,
  Then, Lord, be at my side.

3 O God! forsake me not!
  In danger and in trial,
  Stand Thou to strengthen me,
  Amid the world's denial.
  When fierce temptations near,
  And courage turns to fear,
  Do all that Thou hast willed:
  But ne'er forsake Thy child!

227 One prayer I have—all prayers in one.

C. M.   *"Nevertheless—."*   **Martyrdom.**

JAMES MONTGOMERY, 1825.   HUGH WILSON, 1798.
Har. JOHN B. DYKES, 1861.

1. ONE prayer I have— all prayers in one—When I am whol-ly Thine;

Thy will, my God, Thy will be done, And let that will be mine.

2 All-wise, almighty, and all-good.
  In Thee I firmly trust;
Thy ways, unknown or understood,
  Are merciful and just.

3 May I remember that to Thee
  Whate'er I have I owe;
And back, in gratitude, from me
  May all Thy bounties flow.

4 And tho Thy wisdom takes away,
  Shall I arraign Thy will?
No, let me bless Thy name, and say,
  "The Lord is gracious still."

5 A pilgrim thro the Earth I roam,
  Of nothing long possest;
And all must fail when I go home,
  For this is not my rest.

228

1 To THEE, whose temple is all space,
  Whose altar, Earth, sea, skies,
One chorus let all beings raise!
  All nature's incense rise.

2 If I am right, Thy grace impart
  Still in the right to stay:
If I am wrong, oh, teach my heart
  To find that better way!

3 What conscience dictates to be done,
  Or warns me not to do,
This teach me more than Hell to shun,
  That more than Heaven pursue.

4 Save me alike from foolish pride,
  Or impious discontent,
At aught Thy wisdom hath denied,
  Or aught Thy goodness lent.

5 Teach me to feel another's woe,
   To hide the fault I see;
   That mercy I to others show,
   That mercy show to me.

ALEXANDER POPE, 1738. *Abr.*

229   Jesus! my Saviour, look on me.

8.8.8.4.   " *Thou numberest my wanderings.*"   **Kirkland.**

CHARLOTTE ELLIOTT, 1869. *Abr.*   HUBERT P. MAIN, 1896.

1. JE - SUS! my Sav - iour, look on me; For I am wea - - ry and op - prest,

I come to cast my self on Thee; Thou art my Rest!

Copyright, 1896, by Hubert P. Main.

2 Look down on me for I am weak,
   I feel the toilsome journey's length;
Thine aid omnipotent I seek;
   Thou art my Strength!

3 I am bewildered on my way,
   Dark and tempestuous is the night;
Oh send Thou forth some cheering ray;
   Thou art my Light!

4 I hear the storms around me rise:
   But when I dread th' impending shock,
My spirit to her refuge flies;
   Thou art my Rock!

5 Vain is all human aid for me,
   Helpless I in the darkness grope.
My sole reliance is on Thee;
   Thou art my Hope!

6 Standing alone on Jordan's brink,
   In that tremendous latest strife,
Thou wilt not suffer me to sink;
   Thou art my Life!

7 Thou wilt mine every want supply,
   E'en to the end, whate'er befall;
Thro life, in death, eternally,
   Thou art mine All!

230   Our Heavenly Father, hear.

S. M.   *" They that partake of the benefit are believing and beloved."*   **Thacher.**

JAMES MONTGOMERY, 1825.   From GEORGE F. HANDEL, 1732.

1. Our Heav'n - ly Fa - ther, hear The pray'r we of - fer now.

Thy name be hal - lowed far and near, To Thee all na - tions bow.

2 Thy kingdom come. Thy will
   On Earth be done in love,
As saints and seraphim fulfill
   Thy perfect law above.

3 Our daily bread supply,
   While by Thy word we live.
The guilt of our iniquity
   Forgive, as we forgive.

4 From dark temptation's power
   Our feeble hearts defend.
Deliver in the evil hour,
   And guide us to the end.

5 Thine, then, forever be
   Glory and power divine;
The sceptre, throne, and majesty
   Of Heaven and Earth are Thine.

231

1 JESUS, my strength, my hope,
   On Thee I cast my care!
With humble confidence look up,
   And know Thou hear'st my prayer.

2 I want a true regard,—
   A single, steady, aim,
Unmoved by threat'ning or reward,—
   To Thee and Thy great name.

3 The praying spirit breathe.
   The watching power impart.
From all entanglements beneath,
   Call off my peaceful heart.

4 Suffer'd no more to rove
   O'er all the Earth abroad,
Arrest the pris'ner of Thy love,
   And shut me up in God!

CHARLES WESLEY, 1742. *Abr.*

232 Still, still with Thee, my God!

S. M. *" Of whom shall I be afraid ! "* **Mornington.**

JAMES DRUMMOND BURNS, 1856. GARRATT C. WELLESLEY, 1760.

1. STILL, still with Thee, my God! I would de - light to be;

By day, by night, at home, a - broad, I would be still with Thee.

2 With Thee, when dawn comes in
   And calls me back to care;
   Each day returning to begin
   With Thee, my God! in prayer.

3 With Thee, amid the crowd
   That throngs the busy mart,
   To hear Thy voice, 'mid clamor loud,
   Speak softly to my heart.

4 With Thee, when day is done,
   And evening calms the mind;
   The setting, as the rising, Sun
   With Thee my heart would find.

5 With Thee, in Thee, by faith
   Abiding I would be;
   By day, by night, in life, in death,
   I would be still with Thee!

233

1 JESUS, we look to Thee,
   Thy promised presence claim;
   Thou in the midst of us shalt be,
   Assembled in Thy name.

2 Not in the name of pride
   Or self are we now met:
   From nature's paths we turn aside,
   And wordly thoughts forget.

3 We meet the grace to take,
   Which Thou hast freely given;
   We meet on Earth for Thy dear sake,
   That we may meet in Heaven.

4 Present we know Thou art,
   But, oh, Thyself reveal!
   Now, Lord, let every bounding heart
   Thy mighty comfort feel.

CHARLES WESLEY, 1740. *Abr.*

234   Lord, speak to me, that I may speak.

L. M.   *"That ye may shew forth the excellencies of Him who called you."*   Rose Hill.

FRANCES R. HAVERGAL, 1872. Abr.   JOSEPH E. SWEETSER, 1849.

1. LORD, speak to me, that I may speak In liv - ing ech - oes of Thy tone;

As Thou hast sought, so let me seek Thine err - ing chil - dren, lost and lone.

2 Oh lead me, Lord, that I may lead
    The wandering and the wavering feet.
Oh feed me, Lord, that I may feed
    Thy hungering ones with manna sweet.

3 Oh strengthen me, that while I stand
    Firm on the Rock and strong in Thee,
I may stretch out a loving hand
    To wrestlers with the troubled sea.

4 Oh give Thine own sweet rest to me,
    That I may speak with soothing power
A word in season, as from Thee,
    To weary ones, in needful hour.

5 Oh fill me with Thy fulness, Lord,
    Until my very heart o'erflow
In kindling thought and glowing word,
    Thy love to tell, Thy praise to show.

235

1 REDEEMED from guilt, redeemed from
    My soul at rest and dried my tears, [fears,
What can I do, O Love Divine,—
    What to repay such gifts as Thine?

2 What can I do, so poor, so weak,
    But from Thy hands new blessing seek,—
A heart to feel Thy mercies more,
    A soul to know Thee and adore?

3 Oh teach me at Thy feet to fall,
    And yield Thee up myself, mine all,
Before Thy face my sins to own,
    And live and die to Thee alone!

4 Thy gracious Spirit, Lord, impart,
    Expand, exalt, fill full my heart;
So that a holy life may be
    Some faint return, O Lord, to Thee.

HENRY F. LYTE, 1834.

236 Thou Lord of my life, by the words Thou hast said.

11.9.11.9. *" If any man thirst let Him come unto Me."* **Oland.**

M. W. S., 1887. Swedish Koral, 17th Century. *Abr.*

1. Thou Lord of my life, by the words Thou hast said, I bring Thee the

bur - dens that pain me. Deep wa - ters of sor - row close o - ver my

head, Un - less Thy good hand shall sus - tain.... me. A - men! A - men!

2 O Help of the stricken! O Hope of the lost!
Where else can I go with my crying?
Thou One all-acquainted with grief to Thy cost,
My soul to Thy mercy is flying.

3 Almighty Redeemer, give ear to my prayer!
Uphold me! Abandon me never!
Forgive me my doubts of Thine infinite care.
Enfold me forever and ever. *Amen.*

237 In the hour of trial.

6s & 5s, D.   *"The world passeth away and the lust thereof."*   Spencer Lane.

JAMES MONTGOMERY, 1834.   ENGLISH AIR.

1. In the hour of tri - al, Je-sus, plead for me; Lost by base de - ni - al I depart from Thee;
2. With its witching pleasures Would this vain world charm, Or its sordid treas-ures Spread to work me harm,

When Thou see'st me wav - er, With a look re - call, ... Nor for fear or fa - vor Suf-fer me to fall.
Bring to my re- -mem-brance Sad Geth-sem-a - ne, ... Or, in darker semblance, Cross-crown'd Calvary.

3 If with sore affliction
  Thou in love chastise,
  Pour Thy benediction
  On the sacrifice.
  Then, upon Thine altar
  Freely offered up,
  Tho the flesh may falter,
  Faith shall drain the cup.

4 When in dust and ashes
  To the grave I sink,
  While Heaven's glory flashes
  O'er the shelving brink,
  On Thy truth relying
  Thro that mortal strife,
  Lord, receive me, dying,
  To eternal life!

238 Holding none above Thee.

6s & 5s, D.   *"And the second is like unto it."*   Magdalena.

M. W. S., 1595.   JOHN B. DYKES, 1861.

1. Holding none a-bove Thee, Mind and strength and heart, I my God would love Thee, All for what Thou art.

Consecration.

As Thy first and great-est, Teach me this command, And what Thou createst, Make, in grace to stand.

2 Help me love my neighbor
As Thou loved'st me.
Help me share His labor
In Thy sympathy.
Let Thy Spirit only
All my footsteps bend,
To the faint and lonely,
For Thy sake, a friend.

3 So, as truth and beauty
Make one perfect whole,
Joy shall blend with duty
In my deepest soul.
Blessèd most in giving
What to love belongs,
Mine Thy law of living,
And Thy statutes songs.

239   Oft in danger, oft in woe.

7.7.7.7.   "*Against the world-rulers of this darkness, against the spiritual hosts of wickedness.*"   Clarion.

HENRY KIRKE WHITE, 1804. *Alt.*   EDWARD F. RIMBAULT, 1867.

1. Oft in dan-ger, oft in woe, On-ward, Christ-ian, on-ward go! Fight tho
fight, main-tain the strife, Strengthened with the Bread of life. A - - men, A - men.

2 Onward, Christian, onward go!
Join the war, and face the foe.
Will ye flee in danger's hour?
Know ye not your Captain's power?

3 Let your drooping hearts be glad.
March, in heavenly armor clad.
Fight, nor think the battle long;
Vict'ry soon shall tune your song. *Amen.*

240 Stand up,—stand up for Jesus!

7s & 6s, D.   " *Quit you like men.* "   Ellacombe.

GEORGE DUFFIELD, 1858.
(*The entire and authentic text.*)   ST. GALL GESANGBUCH, 1851.

1. STAND up,—stand up for Je - sus! Ye soldiers of the Cross. Lift high His roy - al ban - ner; It

must not suf-fer loss. From vic-t'ry un - to vic - t'ry His ar-my shall He lead, Till ev - 'ry

foe is vanquish'd And Christ is Lord in-deed.

2 Stand up,—stand up for Jesus!
    The solemn watchword hear.
  If while ye sleep He suffers,
    Away with shame and fear.
  Where'er ye meet with evil,
    Within you or without,
  Charge, for the God of Battles,
    And put the foe to rout.

3 Stand up,—stand up for Jesus!
    The trumpet call obey.
  Forth to the mighty conflict,
    In this His glorious day.
  Ye that are men now serve Him,
    Against unnumber'd foes,
  Let courage rise with danger,
    And strength to strength oppose.

4 Stand up,—stand up for Jesus!
    Stand in His strength alone;
  The arm of flesh will fail you,
    Ye dare not trust your own.
  Put on the Gospel armor,
    Each piece put on with prayer.
  Where duty calls, or danger,
    Be never wanting there!

Consecration.

5 Stand up,—stand up for Jesus!
  Each soldier to his post.
Close up the broken column,
  And shout thro all the host!
Make good the loss so heavy,
  In those that still remain,
And prove to all around you
  That death itself is gain.

6 Stand up,—stand up for Jesus!
  The strife will not be long;
This day the noise of battle,
  The next, the victor's song.
To him that overcometh,
  A crown of life shall be;
He, with the King of Glory,
  Shall reign eternally!

241   O Jesus, I have promised.

7s & 6s, D.   *"The God whose I am, whom also I serve."*   Miriam.

JOHN E. BODE, 1869. *Abr.*   JOSEPH P. HOLBROOK, 1865.

1. O Je-sus, I have prom-ised To serve Thee to the end; Be Thou for-ev-er near me,
D.S.—Nor wan-der from the path-way,

My Mas-ter and my Friend! I shall not fear the bat-tle If Thou art by my side,
If Thou wilt be my Guide.

2 Oh, let me hear Thee speaking
  In accents clear and still,
Above the storms of passion,
  The murmurs of self-will!
Oh, speak to reassure me,
  To hasten or control!
Oh, speak and make me listen,
  Thou Guardian of my soul!

3 O Jesus, Thou hast promised
  To all who follow Thee
That where Thou art in glory
  There shall Thy servant be;
And, Jesus, I have promised
  To serve Thee to the end,—
Oh, give me grace to follow
  My Master and my Friend!

242 Workman of God, oh, lose not heart.

C. M. D.   *"In nothing terrified by your adversaries."*   **Anglia.**

FREDERICK W. FABER, 1849. *Abr.*   AN ENGLISH CAROL.

1. Work - man of God, oh, lose not heart, But learn what God is like; And in the dark-est battle-field Thou shalt know where to strike; Thrice blest is he to whom is giv'n The in - stinct that can tell That God is on the field, when He Is most in - vis - i - ble.

2 God's glory is a wondrous thing,
   Most strange in all its ways,
And of all things on Earth least like
   What men agree to praise;

For right is right, since God is God,
   And right the day must win;
To doubt would be disloyalty,
   To falter would be sin.

243 Saviour, Thou of life the lender.

8.7.8.7.8.7.   *"He that followeth Me shall not walk in darkness."*   **Smith College.**

JOHN BURTON, 1806 (I). *Alt.*   ROBERT SCHUMANN, 1879.
    Arr. BENJAMIN C. BLODGETT, 1885.

1. Saviour! Thou of life the len-der, We would yield our lives to Thee. Thankfully our pow'rs sur-ren-der,

Consecration.

Thine and on-ly Thine to be....... O our Master and De-fend-er, We would serve Thee faithfully.

2 Send us, Lord, where Thou wilt send us,
　　Only do Thou guide our way.
　By Thy grace thro life attend us,
　　Gladly then shall we obey.
　With Thy constant love befriend us
　　All, as children of the day.

3 Write Thy Name upon our foreheads,
　　Write our names upon Thy hand.
　Marching onward with hosannas,
　　In Thine holy pilgrim-band,
　May we in that heavenly country,
　　With Thy ransomed armies stand.

244　　The trumpet call of duty.

7s & 6s, D.　　　　" Buying up the opportunity."　　　　　Petros.

ALFRED H. MILES, Abr.　　　　　　　　　THE LAUSANNE PSALTER.

Energico.

1. THE trumpet call of du-ty Is sounding on the air! It calls for strength and beauty, It calls the brave and fair!

f　　　　　　　　　　*marcato.*

It calls to strife and sor-row, To present toil and pain; But vic-to-ry to-mor-row Shall bring e-ter-nal gain!

2 Wherever pride oppresses,
　　Wherever ills abound,
　Wherever wrong distresses,
　　Our battle-field is found.

Wherever duty calls us,
　　And conscience bids us go,
Whatever else befalls us,
　　We can but triumph know.

Consecration.

Man the life-boat!

8s & 7s, D. With chorus.   *"Whom shall we send? and who will go?"*   Life-Boat.

M. W. S., 1890.   HUBERT P. MAIN, 1890.

1. MAN THE LIFE-BOAT! Man the life-boat! Strong and short above the roar, Sounds the order to the watchers
2. Man the life-boat! Man the life-boat! Fog and night and cruel sea, All the odds of death against them,

On the tem-pest-beat-en shore, Hark! a-gain the guns ap-peal-ing! Sig-nals burn for swift re - lief;
And e - ter - nal jeop-ard - y. Thou, who bid'st us dare the surg-es, Stay us at the struggling oar!

There are men and wives and children, Facing death, on yonder reef! }
Nay, go with us to the res-cue! Shall they sink in sight of shore? } Man the life-boat! Man the life-boat!

Help, for Christ's sake, them that drown! In the per - il of great wa-ters, Let them not go down!

Copyright, 1891, by Hubert P. Main.

Consecration.

3 Man the life-boat! Man the life-boat!
  Courage, fellow men! 'Tis He,
Guiding us to your deliverance,
  Once that trod the Galilee!
Lo, the Church that carrieth Jesus,
  Not death's flood-gates shall o'erwhelm;
Scourging storms but urge us shoreward,
  Life and love are at the helm!

4 Man the life-boat! Man the life-boat!
  Think how once on breaking deck
Thou didst stand aghast, till Jesus
  Brought thee from the lurching wreck.
To the oars then! O Redeemer,
  Let Thy heart thrill every hand,
Till the souls in mortal danger
  Find thro Thee the solid land.

246   Saviour, Blessèd Saviour.

6s & 5s, D.   *" Rejoice in the Lord alway."*   Papworth.

GODFREY THRING, 1862. *Abr.*   EWARD J. HOPKINS, 1870.

1. SAV-IOUR, bless-ed Sav-iour, List-en while we sing, Hearts and voices rais - ing praises to our King.

All we have to of - fer, All we hope to be, Bod - y, soul, and spir - it, All we yield to Thee.

Org. Ped.

2 Higher then, and higher,
  Bear the ransomed soul,
Earthly toils forgotten,
  Saviour, to its goal.
Life has lost its shadows,
  Pure the light within;
Thou hast shed Thy radiance
  On a world of sin.

3 Great, and ever greater,
  Are Thy mercies here;
True and everlasting
  Are the glories there;
Where no pain nor sorrow,
  Toil nor care, is known,
Where the angel legions
  Circle round Thy throne.

247 The Son of God goes forth to war.

C. M.   *"Subdued kingdoms, wrought righteousness, obtained promises."*   **St. Anne.**

REGINALD HEBER, 1827. *Abr.*   WILLIAM CROFT, 1708.

Alla marcia.

1. THE Son of God goes forth to war, A king - ly crown to gain

His blood - red ban - ner streams a - far! Who fol - lows in His train?

2 Who best can drink His cup of woe,
Triumphant over pain,
Who patient bears His cross below,
He follows in His train.

3 A noble army, men and boys,
The matron and the maid,
Around the Saviour's throne rejoice,
In robes of light arrayed.

4 They met the tyrant's brandished steel,
The lion's gory mane,
They bowed their necks the death to feel;—
Who follows in their train?

5 They climbed the steep ascent of Heaven
Thro peril, toil and pain;—
O God, to us may grace be given
To follow in their train!

248

1 O STILL in accents sweet and strong
Sounds forth the ancient word,
"More reapers for white harvest fields,
More laborers for the Lord!"

2 We hear the call, in dreams no more
In selfish ease we lie;
But girded for our Father's work,
Go forth beneath His sky.

3 Where prophets' word, and martyrs' blood,
And prayers of saints were sown,
We, to their labors entering in,
Would reap where they have strown.

4 O Thou whose call our hearts hath stirred!
To do Thy will we come,
Thrust in our sickles at Thy word,
And bear our harvest home.

SAMUEL LONGFELLOW, 1864.

Consecration.

249   Awake my soul! stretch every nerve.

C. M.   *" Let the redeemed of the Lord say so."*   **Azmon.**

PHILIP DODDRIDGE, 1740.   CARL GOTTHILF GLÄSER, 1828.
Arr. LOWELL MASON, 1841.

1. A - WAKE my soul! stretch ev - ery nerve, And press with vig - or on;

A heav'n - ly race de - mands thy zeal, And an im - mor - tal crown.

2 A cloud of witnesses around
Hold thee in full survey;
Forget the steps already trod,
And onward urge thy way.

3 'Tis God's all-animating voice
That calls thee from on high.
'Tis His own hand presents the prize
To thine aspiring eye.

4 That prize with peerless glories bright,
Which shall new lustre boast,
When victors' wreaths and monarchs' gems
Shall blend in common dust.

5 Blest Saviour, introduced by Thee,
Have I my race begun ;
And, crowned with victory, at Thy feet
I'll lay my honors down.

250

1 ROBBED, bruised and dying, once I lay,
Upon a lonely road,
When One came journeying on His way,
And wondrous mercy showed!

2 He saw me, pitied, came and bound,
And bore me to the inn,
Cared wisely for mine every wound,
As He were very kin.

3 He watched beside me all the night,
Till dawn did comfort bring ;
Went only when 't was fully light,
And paid my reckoning.

4 So now, to keep the vows I made
Beneath those glowing eyes,
I would my fallen fellow aid,
And go and do likewise.

M. W. S., 1886.

251 Lord, as to Thy dear Cross we flee.

C. M. *"That I may show him the kingdom of God."* **St. Agnes.**

JOHN H GURNEY, 1838. JOHN B. DYKES, 1858.

1. Lord, as to Thy dear Cross we flee And plead to be for - given,

So let Thy life our pat - tern be And form our souls for Heaven.

2 Help us, thro good report and ill,
Our daily cross to bear,
Like Thee to do our Father's will,
Our brethren's griefs to share.

3 Let grace our selfishness expel,
Our earthliness refine,
And kindness in our bosoms dwell,
As free and true as Thine.

4 Should friends misjudge or foes defame
Or brethren faithless prove,
Then, like Thine own, be all our aim
To conquer them by love.

5 Kept peaceful in the midst of strife,
Forgiving and forgiven,
Oh may we lead the pilgrim's life
And follow Thee to Heaven!

252

1 TAKE, Lord, the little I can do;
For love counts nothing small,
And lowly service serveth true
In gladly giving all.

2 To stay one weary heart in pain,
One cheering word to say,
To help one sufferer sing again,
Sufficeth for the day.

3 In simple errands, silent praise,
And pure obedience trod,
So, one by one, shall all my days
Be hid with Christ in God.

4 Pavilioned safe from human strife
In sweet society,
No accident can touch my life;
Its treasures are with Thee!

M. W. S., 1890.

Consecration.

253   Oh, for a heart to praise my God.

C. M.   *" Ye have purified your souls in your obedience to the truth."*   **Tudor.**

CHARLES WESLEY, 1742.   JOHN MARBECKE'S BOOK, 1550.
Har. HENRY J. GAUNTLETT, 1846.

1. Oh, for a heart to praise my God, A heart from sin set free,

A heart that's sprinkled with the blood . So free - ly shed for me!

2 A heart resigned, submissive, meek,
My dear Redeemer's throne,
Where only Christ is heard to speak,
Where Jesus reigns alone!

3 A humble, lowly, contrite heart,
Believing, true and clean!
Which neither life nor death can part
From Him that dwells within.

4 A heart in every thought renewed
And filled with love divine,
Perfect and right and pure and good,
A copy, Lord, of Thine!

5 Thy nature, gracious Lord, impart!
Come quickly from above,
Write Thy new name upon my heart,—
Thy new, best name of love.

254

1 LORD in this dust Thy sovereign voice
First quickened love divine.
I am all Thine, Thy care and choice,
My very praise is Thine.

2 I praise Thee, while Thy providence
In childhood frail I trace,
For blessings giv'n ere dawning sense
Could seek or scan Thy grace.

3 Blessings in boyhood's marv'ling hour,
Bright dreams and fancyings strange;
Blessings when reason's awful power
Gave thought a bolder range.

4 And such Thy tender force be still,
When self would swerve or stray,
Shaping to truth the froward will
Along Thy narrow way.

JOHN HENRY NEWMAN, 1829. *Abr.*

255 Almighty Lord, with one accord.

C. M.   *"This is My covenant which ye shall keep, between Me and you, and thy seed after thee."*   Evan.

M. W. S., 1896.

CELTIC MELODY.
Arr. WILLIAM H. HAVERGAL, 1846.

1. AL - MIGHT - Y   Lord,   with   one   ac - cord,   We   of - fer   Thee   our   youth,

And   pray   that   Thou   would'st give   us   now   The   war - fare   of   the   truth.

256

2 Thy cause doth claim our souls by name,
   Thereto Thou makest strong;
In all the land, one steadfast band,
   May we to Christ belong.

3 Let fall on every College hall
   The lustre of Thy cross,
So love shall dare Thy work to share
   And count all else as loss.

4 Our hearts be ruled, our spirits schooled,
   Alone Thy will to seek,
And where we find Thy holy mind,
   Instruct our lips to speak.

5 With conscience pure and purpose sure
   May we do all; and then—
No more in part, but as Thou art,
   Know Thee, our Lord! Amen.

1 By all true sons who've loved these walls,
   The living and the dead,
We sing our happy College halls
   And days too quickly sped.

2 Thy smile, O God of wisdom, still
   Enlarge all labors here,
Let joy Thy gracious plans fulfil
   With every ampler year.

3 Let generous hope and high behest
   These brightening ways adorn,—
Our Mother's ancient honor rest
   On children yet unborn.

4 What toil and trust whilere begun
   Increase from more to more,
Till all the tasks of Time are done
   And Man's long march is o'er.

M. W. S., 1896.

Consecration.

Onward, Christian soldiers!

6s & 5s. *"By the armor of righteousness."* **St. Gertrude.**

S. Baring-Gould, 1865. *Abr.* Arthur S. Sullivan, 1872.

Con moto.

1. ON - WARD, Christian sol - diers, March-ing as to war, With the Cross of Je - sus
2. Like a might-y arm - y, Moves the Church of God; Brothers, we are tread-ing

Go - ing on be - fore! Christ, the roy-al Mas - ter, Leads a-gainst the foe; For-ward in - to
Where the saints have trod. We are not di - vid - ed, All one bod-y we, One in hope, in

mf

bat - tle See His ban-ners go. *Onward, Christian sol - diers, Marching as to war,*
doc - trine, One in char - i - ty.

With the Cross of Je - sus Go - ing on be - fore!

3 Crowns and thrones may perish,
   Kingdoms rise and wane,
   But the Church of Jesus
   Constant will remain:
   Gates of hell can never
   'Gainst that Church prevail;
   We have Christ's own promise,
   And that cannot fail.
   Onward, etc.

258   Lord, Thou hast taught our hearts to glow.

C. M.   *" They that partake of the benefit are believing and beloved."*   Dundee.

RAY PALMER, 1865.   ANDRO HART'S PSALTER, 1615.

1 LORD, Thou hast taught our hearts to
     With love's undying flame; [glow
     But more of Thee we long to know,
     And more would love Thy name.

2 Thy life, Thy death, inspire our song,
     Thy Spirit breathes thro all,
     And here our feet would linger long:
     But we obey Thy call.

3 Thou bid'st us go, with Thee to stand
     Against Hell's marshalled powers;
     And heart to heart, and hand to hand,
     To make Thine honor ours.

4 With Thine own pity, Saviour, see
     The thronged and darkening way;
     We go to win the lost to Thee,
     Oh help us, Lord, we pray!

5 Teach Thou our lips of Thee to speak,
     Of Thy sweet love to tell;
     Till they who wander far shall seek
     And find and serve Thee well.

6 O'er all the world Thy Spirit send,
     And make Thy goodness known,
     Till Earth and Heaven together blend
     Their praises at Thy throne.

259   A charge to keep I have.

S. M.   *" If by the Spirit ye mortify the deeds of the body, ye shall live."*   Aston.

CHARLES WESLEY, 1762.   JOHN HEYWOOD.
            (last stanza.)

1. A CHARGE to keep I have,—A God to glo-ri - fy, A nev-er-dy - ing soul to save, And fit it for the sky.

2 To serve the present age,
     My calling to fulfill;
     Oh may it all my powers engage
     To do my Master's will!

3 Arm me with jealous care,
     As in Thy sight to live;

And oh, Thy servant, Lord, prepare
     A strict account to give!

4 Help me to watch and pray,
     And on Thyself rely!
     Assured if I my trust betray,
     I shall forever die.

Consecration.

260   Soldiers of Christ, arise.

S. M.   *" First they gave their own selves to the Lord."*   **St. Augustine.**

CHARLES WESLEY, 1749. *Abr.*   JOHN SEB. BACH.

1. SOLDIERS of Christ, a - rise   Strong in the strength which God supplies
And gird your armor on,   Thro His e - ter - nal Son.

2 Stand, then, in His great might,
  With all His strength endued,
And take, to arm you for the fight,
  The panoply of God.

3 From strength to strength go on;
  Wrestle, and fight, and pray;
Tread all the powers of darkness down,
  And win the well-fought day.

261   We give Thee but Thine own.

S. M.   *" Love ye therefore the strangers, for ye were strangers."*   **Dennis.**

WILLIAM W. HOW, 1854. *Abr.*   JOHANN GEORG NAGELI, 1790.

1 WE give Thee but Thine own,
  Whate'er the gift may be,
All that we have is Thine alone,
  A trust, O Lord, from Thee;

2 Lo! hearts are bruised and dead,
  And homes are bare and cold;
And lambs, for whom the Shepherd bled,
  Are straying from the fold.

3 To comfort and to bless,
  To find a balm for woe,
To tend the lone and fatherless
  Is angels' work below.

4 And we believe Thy word,
  Tho dim our faith may be;
Whate'er for Thine we do, O Lord,
  We do it unto Thee.

Consecration.

262   Like the eagle, upward, onward.

8s & 7s.   *"According as each hath received a gift, ministering it"*   **Stockwell.**

HORATIUS BONAR, 1856. *Abr.*   DARIUS E. JONES, 1846.

1. LIKE the ea - gle, up - ward, on - ward, Let my soul in faith be borne.

Calm - ly gaz - ing, sky - ward, sun - ward, Let mine eyes re - flect the morn.

2 Where the Cross, God's love revealing,
   Sets the fettered spirit free,
Where it sheds its wondrous healing,
   There, my soul, thy rest shall be!

3 Oh, may I, no longer dreaming,
   Idly waste my golden day;
But, each precious hour redeeming,
   Upward, onward press my way!

263   Jesus calls us, o'er the tumult.

8s & 7s.   *"Not a hearer that forgetteth: but a doer that worketh."*   **New Jersey.**

CECIL F. ALEXANDER, 1852.   WALTER B. GILBERT, 1870.

1. JE - SUS calls us, o'er the tum - ult Of our life's wild, rest - less sea.

Consecration.

Day by day His sweet voice sound - eth Say - ing, 'Chris-tian fol - low Me.'

2 As, of old, disciples heard it
   By the Galilean lake,
   Turned from home and toil and kindred,
   Leaving all for His dear sake;

3 In our joys and in our sorrows,
   Days of toil and hours of ease,
   Still He calls, in cares and pleasures,
   That we love Him more than these.

4 Jesus calls us from the worship
   Of the vain world's golden store,
   From each idol that would keep us,
   Saying, 'Christian, love Me more.'

5 Jesus calls us; by Thy mercies,
   Saviour, make us hear Thy call,
   Give our hearts to Thine obedience,
   Serve and love Thee best of all.

264   Courage, brother, do not stumble.

8s & 7s.   *" Gird up thy loins."*   Louise.
NORMAN MACLEOD, *Abr.*   HUBERT P. MAIN, 1869.

Copyright, 1869, by Biglow & Main.

1 COURAGE, brother, do not stumble,
   Tho thy path be dark as night.
   There's a star to guide the humble,—
   Trust in God and do the right.

2 Perish policy and cunning,
   Perish all that fears the light,
   Whether losing, whether winning,
   Trust in God and do the right.

3 Trust no party, sect, or faction;
   Trust no leaders in the fight;

But in every word and action
Trust in God and do the right.

4 Trust no lovely forms of passion;
   Fiends may look like angels bright;
   Trust no custom, school, or fashion,
   Trust in God and do the right.

5 Some will hate thee, some will love thee,
   Some will flatter, some will slight.
   Cease from man and look above thee,
   Trust in God and do the right.

265

Lord, every day and everywhere.

L. M.
M. W. S., 1387. *Abr.*

"The God of hope fill you with all joy and peace in believing."

Medway.
Giovanni B. Pergolesi, 1730.

1. Lord, ev-ery day and ev-ery-where, In ev-ery way, or large or least,
Let faith-ful ser - vice be in-creased, And Thine ap - prov-al be my care.

2 Let all my plans be simplified
To follow Thee at small remove,
To catch the secret of that love
Which drew the needy to Thy side.

3 Control the quick, impatient speech,
Curb my fierce pride and selfishness,
Enjoin my thought to heal and bless,
First let me learn the thing I teach.

4 I would not bring Thee what is lame,
Unseemly, torn, what cost me naught:
But, by Thy patient grace besought,
Would mark my best with Thy dear name.

5 Put mine with Thine in perfect chord,
Forgiveness let me ne'er forget:
Bend Thine ear lower.—Love me yet!
I ask no more, what could I, Lord?

266

1 O Master, let me walk with Thee
In lowly paths of service free.
Tell me Thy secret. Help me bear
The strain of toil, the fret of care.

2 Help me the slow of heart to move
By some clear winning word of love.
Teach me the wayward feet to stay,
And guide them in the homeward way.

3 Teach me Thy patience; still with Thee
In closer, dearer company,
In work that keeps faith sweet and strong,
In trust that triumphs over wrong.

4 In hope that sends a shining ray
Far down the future's broadening way,
In peace that only Thou canst give,
With Thee, O Master, let me live!

Washington Gladden, 1879. *Abr.*

267   Rise, my soul, and stretch thy wings.

7s & 6s, P.   *" Fully assured in all the will of God."*   **Amsterdam.**

ROBERT SEAGRAVE, 1742.   AD. BY JAMES NARES, 1750.

1. Rise, my soul, and stretch thy wings, Thy bet - ter por - tion trace;
   Rise from trans-i - to - ry things Toward Heav'n, thy native place. Sun and moon and stars de - cay,

Time shall soon this Earth re - move; Rise, my soul, and haste a - way To seats pre-pared a - bove.

2 Rivers to the ocean run,
  Nor stay in all their course.
Fire, ascending, seeks the Sun.
  Both speed them to their source.
So a soul, that's born of God,
  Pants to view His glorious face,
Upwards tends to His abode,
  To rest in His embrace.

3 Fly me, riches, fly me, cares,
  While I that coast explore;
Flatt'ring world, with all thy snares
  Solicit me no more!
Pilgrims fix not here their home;
  Strangers tarry but a night;
When the last dear morn is come,
  They'll rise to joyful light.

4 Cease, ye pilgrims, cease to mourn,
  Press onward to the prize;
Soon our Saviour will return
  Triumphant in the skies.
Yet a season, and you know
  Happy entrance will be given,
All our sorrows left below,
  And Earth exchanged for Heaven.

268

To THE CROSS, Thine altar, bind
  Me with the cords of love;
Never let me freedom find
  From Thee, my Lord, to move:
That I never, never more
  From my loving Master part,
To the posts of mercy's door,
  Oh, nail my willing heart!

CHARLES WESLEY, 1745. *Abr.*

Consecration.

269   Take my life, and let it be.

7.7.7.7.   *" We may have a strong encouragement."*   **Lubeck.**

FRANCES R. HAVERGAL, 1873. *Abr.*   JOHANN ANAST. FREYLINGHAUSEN, 1704.

1. TAKE my life, and let it be Con - se - crat - ed, Lord, to Thee;

Take my mo - ments and my days, Let them flow in cease - less praise.

2 Take my feet, and let them be
Swift and beautiful for Thee;
Take my hands and let them move
At the impulse of Thy love.

3 Take my lips and let them be
Filled with messages from Thee;
Take my voice and let me sing
Always, only, for my King.

4 Take my silver and my gold;
Not a mite would I withhold.
Take my will and make it Thine;
It shall be no longer mine.

5 Take my heart, it *is* Thine own!
It shall be Thy royal throne.
Take myself, and I will be,
Ever, only, all!—for Thee.

270   While the Sun is shining.

6s & 5s, D.   *"I have meat to eat that ye know not."*   **Noonday.**

THOMAS A. STOWELL. *Abr.*   WILLIAM H. MONK, 1861.

1. WHILE the Sun is shin-ing Brightly in the sky, Ere his rays de - clin-ing Tell that night is nigh;

rit.

Ere the shad-ows fall-ing, Lengthen on our way, Hark! a voice is call-ing, "Work while it is day."

2 Work, but not in sadness,
For your Lord above;
He will make it gladness
With His smile of love.

When that Lord returning
Knocketh at the gate,
Let your lights be burning,
Be like men who wait.

271 Without haste and without rest.

7·7·7·7·7·7.
ANON, based upon GOETHE's "*Ohne Hast, Ohne Rast.*"

"*They turned not as they went.*"

Dix.
CONRAD KOCHER, 1838.

1 "WITHOUT haste and without rest,"—
Bind the motto to thy breast.
Bear it with thee as a spell,—
Storm and sunshine, guard it well.
Heed not flowers that round thee bloom,
Bear it onward to the tomb.

2 Haste not! Let no thoughtless deed
Mar for aye the spirit's speed.
Ponder well and know the right,
Onward then with all thy might.
Haste not! Years can ne'er atone
For one reckless action done.

3 Rest not! Life is sweeping by;
Go and dare before you die.
Something mighty and sublime
Leave behind to conquer time!
Glorious 'tis to live for aye,
When these forms have past away.

4 Haste not! Rest not! Calmly wait,
Meekly bear the storms of fate.
Duty be thy polar guide.
Do the right whate'er betide.
Haste not! Rest not! Conflicts past,
God shall crown thy work at last.

Consecration.

272   Awake, our souls! away, our fears!

L. M.   *" He that voucheth for me is on high."*   **Seasons.**

ISAAC WATTS, 1707. *Abr.*   IGNACE PLEYEL, 1790.

1. A - WAKE, our souls! a - way, our fears! Let ev - ery trem-bling thought be gone;

A - wake, and run the heaven - ly race, And put a cheer - ful cour - age on.

2 True,—'t is a strait and thorny road,
And mortal spirits tire and faint:
But they forget the mighty God,
Who feeds the strength of every saint.

3 The mighty God! whose matchless power
Is ever new and ever one,
And firm endures while endless years
Their everlasting circles run.

273   O God! we praise Thee and confess.

C. M.   *" Give praise to our God all ye His servants."*   **St. Saviour.**

The TE DEUM, 4th Century, A. D.   FREDERICK G. BAKER, 1872.
Arr. TATE BRADY, 1703

1. O GOD! we praise Thee, and confess That Thou the on-ly Lord And ev - er-last-ing Fa-ther art, By all the Earth a-dored!

2 To Thee, all angels cry aloud;
To Thee the powers on high,
Both cherubim and seraphim,
Continually do cry,—

3 O Holy, Holy, Holy Lord,
Whom heavenly hosts obey,
The world is with the glory filled
Of Thy majestic sway!

The Church.

4 Th' apostles' glorious company,
  And prophets crowned with light,
  With all the martyrs' noble host,
  Thy constant praise recite.

5 The holy Church thro all the world,
  O Lord, confesses Thee,
  That Thou th' Eternal Father art,
  Of boundless majesty.

274   Not worthy, Lord, to gather up the crumbs.

10.10.10.10.   *"This Man receiveth sinners and eateth with them."*   Meridian.

EDWARD H. BICKERSTETH, 1870. *Abr.*   M. W. S., 1885.

1. Not wor-thy, Lord, to gath-er up the crumbs, With trembling hand, that from Thy table fall,

A wea-ry heav - y - la-den sinner comes, To plead Thy promise and obey Thy call. A - men.

Copyright 1886, by Biglow & Main.

2 I am not worthy to be thought Thy child,
  Nor sit the last and lowest at Thy board.
  Too long a wand'rer and too oft beguiled,
  I only ask one reconciling word.

3 I hear Thy voice; Thou bid'st me come and rest;
  I come, I kneel, I clasp Thy piercèd feet!
  Thou bid'st me take my place, a welcome guest,
  Among Thy saints, and of Thy banquet eat.

4 My praise can only breathe itself in prayer,
  My prayer can only lose itself in Thee,
  Dwell Thou forever in my heart, and there,
  Lord! let me sup with Thee,- sup Thou with me. *Amen.*

𝕮𝖍𝖊 𝕮𝖍𝖚𝖗𝖈𝖍.

275　　Bread of the world, in mercy broken.

9.8.9.8.　　　　"Is it not a communion of the blood of Christ?"　　　Grace Church.
REGINALD HEBER, 1827.　　　　　　　　　　　　　　　　　　IGNACE PLEYEL. Arr.

1. BREAD of the world, in mer - cy brok - en, Wine of the soul, in mer - cy shed,

By whom the words of life were spok - en, And in whose death our sins are dead!

2　Look on the hearts by sorrow broken,
　　Look on the tears by sinners shed;
　　And be Thy feast to us the token
　　That by Thy grace our souls are fed.

276　　Many centuries have fled.

7.7.7.7.7.7.　　　　"My glory and the lifter up of my head."　　　Spanish Hymn.
JOSIAH CONDER, 1836. Abr.　　　　　　　　　　　　　Arr. by BENJAMIN CARR, 1824.
　　　　　　　　　　　　　　　　　　　　　　　　　　　　　　FINE.

1. MA - NY cen - tu - ries have fled　Since our Sav - iour broke the bread.
D. C.—Those His bod - y who dis - cern, Thus shall meet till His re - turn.

The Church.

D. C.

And this sa - cred feast or - dained, Ev - er by His Church re - tained.

2 Thro the Church's long eclipse,
When from priest or pastor's lips
Truth divine was never heard,—
'Mid the famine of the word,
Still these symbols witness gave
To His love who died to save.

3 All who bear the Saviour's name,
Here their common faith proclaim;
Tho diverse in tongue or rite,
Here, One Body we unite;
Breaking thus one mystic bread,
Members of one common Head.

277 According to Thy gracious word.

C. M.
JAMES MONTGOMERY, 1825. Abr.

"Thy comforts delight my soul."

St. John.
JAMES TURLE, 1862.

mf   p

1. ACCORDING to Thy gracious word, In meek hu-mil - i - ty, This will I do, my dy-ing Lord, I will re - mem-ber Thee.

278

2 Thy body, broken for my sake,
My bread from Heaven shall be;
Thy testamental cup I take,
And thus remember Thee.

3 Remember Thee, and all Thy pains,
And all Thy love to me?—
Yea, while a breath, a pulse remains,
Will I remember Thee!

4 And when these failing lips grow dumb,
And mind and memory flee,
When Thou shalt in Thy kingdom come,
Then, Lord, remember me!

1 LORD, may the spirit of this feast—
The earnest of Thy love—
Maintain a dwelling in each breast,
Until we meet above.

2 The healing sense of pardoned sin,
The hope that never tires,
The strength a pilgrim's race to win,
The joy that Heaven inspires.

3 Still may their light our duties trace
In lines of hallowed flame,
Like that upon the prophet's face,
When from the mount he came.

LYDIA H. SIGOURNEY, 1845.

279 The Church's one Foundation.

7s & 6s, D. *" Here is the patience of the saints."* **Aurelia.**

Samuel J. Stone, 1866. Abr. Samuel Sed. Wesley, 1864.

1. The Church's one Foun-da-tion, Is Je-sus Christ her Lord. She is His new cre-

a-tion, By wa-ter and the word, From Heav'n He came and sought her, To be His

ho-ly Bride. With His own blood He bought her, And for her life He died. A-men.

2 Elect from every nation,
　Yet one o'er all the Earth,
　Her charter of salvation
　One Lord, one faith, one birth,
　One holy Name she blesses,
　Partakes one holy food,
　And to one hope she presses,
　With every grace endued.

3 The Church shall never perish!
　The dear Lord to defend,
　To guide, sustain and cherish,
　Is with her to the end.
　Tho there be those who hate her
　And false sons in her pale,
　Against or foe or traitor
　She ever shall prevail.

The Church.

4 Tho with a scornful wonder
    Men see her sore opprest,
    By schisms rent far asunder,
    By heresies distrest:
    Yet saints their watch are keeping,
    Their cry goes up, "How long?"
    And soon the night of weeping
    Shall be the morn of song!

5 Mid toil and tribulation,
    And tumult of her war,
    She waits the consummation
    Of peace for evermore,
    Till with the vision glorious
    Her longing eyes are blest,
    And the great Church victorious
    Shall be the Church at rest. *Amen.*

280   When Israel, of the Lord beloved.

L. M.   *" With good courage we say—The Lord is my helper!"*   **Humility.**

WALTER, SCOTT, 1820. *Abr.*   SAMUEL PARKMAN TUCKERMAN, 1843.

1. WHEN Is-rael, of the Lord be-loved, Out from the land of bond-age came,

Her fa-thers' God be-fore her moved, An aw-ful guide, in smoke and flame.

2 By day, along th' astonished lands,
    The cloudy pillar glided slow;
    By night, Arabia's crimsoned sands
    Returned the fiery column's glow.

3 There rose the choral hymn of praise,
    And trump and timbrel answered keen,
    And Zion's daughters poured their lays,
    With priests' and warriors' voice between.

4 Lord, present still, tho now unseen,
    When brightly shines the prosp'rous day,
    Be thoughts of Thee a cloudy screen,
    To temper the deceitful ray.

5 And Oh, when gathers on our path,
    In shade and storm, the frequent night,
    Be Thou long-suffering, slow to wrath,
    A burning and a shining light!

281 Oh! where are kings and empires now.

C. M.
Arthur Cleveland Coxe, 1836.

" Until He come whose right it is."

Mear.
Author Unknown, cir. 1726. Alt.

1 Oh! where are kings and empires now,
Of old that went and came?
But, Lord! Thy Church is praying yet,
A thousand years the same.

2 We mark her goodly battlements,
And her foundations strong,
We hear within the solemn voice
Of her unending song.

3 For, not like kingdoms of the world,
Thy holy Church, O God!
Tho earthquake shocks are threat'ning her,
And tempests are abroad.

4 Unshaken as eternal hills,
Immovable she stands,
A mountain that shall fill the Earth,—
A house not made by hands.

282 Blest be the tie that binds.

S. M.
John Fawcett, 1772. Abr.

" Sorrowing most of all that they should behold his face no more."

Boylston.
Lowell Mason, 1832.

1. Blest be the tie that binds Our hearts in Christian love; The fel-low-ship of kindred minds Is like to that a - bove.

2 Before our Father's throne
We pour our ardent prayers;
Our fears, our hopes, our aims are one,
Our comforts and our cares.

3 From sorrow, toil and pain
And sin, we shall be free;
And perfect love and friendship reign
Thro all eternity.

283 Let our choirs new anthems raise!

7s & 6s, P.   *" That they might obtain a better resurrection."*   **Laurel.**

Gk. JOSEPH OF THE STUDIUM, 860.
Tr. JOHN M. NEALE, 1863.

JOSEPH BARNBY, 1868.

1. LET our choirs new an - thems raise! Wake the song of glad - ness! God Him-self to

joy and praise Turns the mar-tyr's sad - ness. Bright the day that won their crown,

Opened Heaven's bright portal, As they laid the mortal down, To put on th'im-mor - tal.

2 Never flinched they from the flame
From the torture, never,
Vain the foeman's sharpest aim,
Satan's best endeavor;
For by faith they saw the land
Decked in all its glory,
Where triumphant now they stand
With the victor's story.

3 Up and follow, Christian men,
Press thro toil and sorrow!
Spurn the night of fear, and then,
Oh, the glorious morrow!
Who will venture on the strife?
Who will first begin it?
Who will seize the Land of Life?
Warriors, up and win it!

286 Blessèd are the sons of God.

7.7.7.7.7.7.
JOSEPH HUMPHREYS, 1743.

"*Who was I that I could withstand God?*"

Rosefield.
CÆSAR MALAN, 1830.

1. { BLESS - ED are the sons of God, They are bought with Je - sus' blood. }
{ They are ran - somed from the grave, Life e - ter - nal they shall have. }

With them num - bered may we be, Here and in E - ter - ni - ty.

2 They are justified by grace,
They enjoy the Saviour's peace.
All their sins are washed away,
They shall stand in God's great day.
With them numbered may we be,
Here and in Eternity.

3 They are lights upon the Earth,—
Children of a heavenly birth.
One with God, with Jesus one,
Glory is in them begun.
With them numbered may we be,
Here and in Eternity.

287 God is the Refuge of His saints.

L. M.
ISAAC WATTS, 1719. *Abr.*

"*Seeking the wealth of His people and speaking peace to all His seed.*"

Ward.
Old Scotch Air.
Arr. LOWELL MASON, 1830.

1. God is the Ref - uge of His saints, When storms of sharp dis - tress in - vade;

Ere we can of-fer our com-plaints, Be - hold Him pres - ent with His aid.

2 Let mountains from their seats be hurled
  Down to the deep, and buried there;
  Convulsions shake the solid world;
  Our faith shall never yield to fear.

3 Loud may the troubled ocean roar:
  In sacred peace our souls abide,
  While every nation, every shore,
  Trembles, and dreads the swelling tide.

288   My trust is in the Lord.

6.6.6.6.8.8.   *"The upright shall behold His face."*   **Christ Church.**

HENRY F. LYTE 1834. *Abr.*   CHARLES STEGGALL, 1865.

1. My trust is in the Lord, What foe can in - jure me? Why bid me like a bird Be-

f *steadily.*

fore the fowl - er flee? The Lord is on His heav'nly throne, And He will shield and save His own.

2 The wicked may assail,
  The tempter sorely try,
  All Earth's foundations fail,
  All nature's springs be dry;
  Yet God is in His holy shrine,
  And I am strong while He is mine.

3 His foes a season here
  May triumph and prevail;
  But ah! the hour is near
  When all their hopes must fail;
  While, like the Sun, His saints shall rise,
  And shine with Him above the skies.

289   Quicken, Lord, our pilgrim going.

8s.7s.6s.5s. P.   *"The shout of a King is among them."*   **"Ein is noth."**

M. W. S., 1884.   Darmstadt Gesangbuch, 1698.

1. Quick - en, Lord, our pil - grim go - ing, Mind - ful of that Fa - ther - land,
Whence Thy prom - ised light is glow - ing, Where Thy true con - fess - ors stand.

Love's ban - ner be - fore us; Truth's fir - ma - ment o'er us; Such faith Thou hast

grant - ed, Our hope is un - daunt - ed. Our boast is right roy - al, — The

God - head Tri - une! The land of the loy - al Will wel - come us soon.

2 Take, O Christ, our full confession!
  Thou that City hast prepared
  For the Church's sure possession,
  Who Thy wayfare now have shared.
  Thy lone path we're wending:
  But shadows are rending.
  We drink of Thy chalice,—
  We'll stand in Thy palace,
  To Thee yield our laurels,
  One jubilee blend
  In Heaven-wide chorals,
  That world without end.

3 On we press with steady marches,
  Sober vigils, joyful cheers;
  Nearer gleam those jewelled arches,
  Just before are Heaven's frontiers.
  Hell's armies may mock us,—
  Their hate shall not baulk us;
  We fear not their leaguer:
  But *on!* true and eager.
  Exalted each valley,
  Each mountain made low,
  In confident rally
  Right homeward we go!

290   O Rock of Ages, one Foundation.

9.8.9.8.   "*That Rock was Christ.*"   Sacrament.
HENRY ARTHUR MARTIN, 1871. *Abr.*   EDWARD J. HOPKINS, 1880.

1. O Rock of A - ges, one Foun - da - tion, On which the liv - ing Church doth rest,—

The Church, whose walls are strong sal - va - tion, Whose gates are praise,—Thy name be blest!

2 Son of the living God! O call us
  Once and again to follow Thee;
  And give us strength, whate'er befall us,
  Thy true disciples still to be.

3 And if our coward hearts deny Thee,
  In inmost thought, in deed, or word,
  Let not our hardness still defy Thee;
  But with a look subdue us, Lord.

291   Christse for the world, we sing.

"The Lord God will cause righteousness and praise to spring forth before all the nations."

6s & 4s.   **New Haven.**
SAMUEL WOLCOTT, 1869. *Abr.*   THOMAS HASTINGS, 1832.

1. CHRIST for the world, we sing. The world to Christ we bring, With lov-ing zeal, The poor and them that mourn, The faint and o - ver-borne, Sin - sick and sor - row-worn, Whom Christ doth heal.

2 Christ for the world, we sing.
The world to Christ we bring.
With one accord;
With us the work to share,

With us reproach to dare,
With us the cross to bear,
For Christ our Lord.

292   I will lift up mine eyes unto the hills.

"That ye may stand perfect and fully assured in all the will of God."

Double Chant.   **Robinson's Chant**
PSALM CXXI : 1—4.   JOHN ROBINSON, 1740.

(a.)   *(b.)*

1 *(a.)* I WILL lift up mine eyes | unto ·· the | hills, || From | whence shall | my help | come? ||
  (b.) My help cometh | from the | Lord || Which | made— | Heaven ·· and | Earth.

2 *(a.)* He will not suffer thy | foot ·· to be | moved; || He that | keepeth ·· thee | will not |
  (b.) Behold, He that | keepeth | Israel || Shall neither | slumber | nor— | sleep. [slumber. ||

293 Hail to the Lord's Anointed.

7s & 6s, D. *"The isles shall wait for His law."* **Webb.**

JAMES MONTGOMERY, 1822. *Abr.* GEORGE JAMES WEBB, 1830.

1. HAIL to the Lord's An-ointed, Great David's greater Son! Hail, in the time ap-pointed, His
D.S.—To take a-way transgression, And

reign on Earth be - gun! He comes to break op - pres - sion, To set the cap - tive free,
rule in e - qui - ty.

2 He comes, with succor speedy,
To those who suffer wrong,
To help the poor and needy,
And bid the weak be strong,
To give them songs for sighing,
Their darkness turn to light,
Whose souls, condemned and dying,
Were precious in His sight.

3 He shall come down, like showers
Upon the fruitful Earth,
And joy and hope, like flowers,
Spring in His path to birth.
The tide of time shall never
His covenant remove;
His name shall stand for ever;
That name to us is—Love.

294

1 LORD of the living harvest,
That whitens o'er the plain,
Where angels soon shall gather
Their sheaves of golden grain,
Accept these hands to labor,
These hearts to trust and love,
And deign with them to hasten
Thy kingdom from above.

2 As laborers in Thy vineyard,
Forth send us, Christ, to be
Content to bear the burden
Of weary days for Thee,
Content to ask no wages,
When Thou shalt call us home,
But to have shared the travail
Which makes Thy kingdom come.

JOHN S. B. MONSELL, 1862. *Abr.*

Missions.

295   On the mountain's top appearing.

8s, 7s & 4.   *"In all the world bearing fruit and increasing."*   **Zion.**

THOMAS KELLY, 1806. *Abr.*

THOMAS HASTINGS, 1830.
Har. HUBERT P. MAIN, 1886.

1. On the mountain's top ap - pear-ing, Lo! the sa - cred her - ald stands,
Welcome news to Zi - on bear-ing—Zi - on, long in hos - tile lands; Mourning cap-tive!

God Him - self shall loose thy bands; Mourning cap - tive! God Him-self shall loose thy bands.

2 Every human tie may perish,
　Friend to friend unfaithful prove,
Mothers cease their own to cherish,
　Heaven and Earth at last remove:
　　But no changes
　Can attend Jehovah's love.

3 In the furnace God may prove thee,
　Thence to bring thee forth more bright:
But can never cease to love thee;
　Thou art precious in His sight.
　　God is with thee—
　God, thine everlasting Light.

296   God speed the gospel!

11.10.11.10.   *"As Thou didst send Me into the world, even so sent I them into the world."*   **Wesley.**

M. W. S., 1890.

LOWELL MASON, 1830.

1. GOD speed the gos-pel! O Fa-ther, in pit - y, Help! where the throngs of the peo-ple are met.

Mississions.

Thro Him who wept o'er the rec - re -ant cit - y. Strengthen our hands for the work Thou hast set.

2 God speed the gospel! By mercies and wonders
   Long hast Thou called us in truth to be free;
   Still let Thy voice, or in whispers or thunders,
   Summon our country to glorify Thee.

3 God speed the gospel! Let uttermost nation
   Hear in the language wherein they were born.
   Send Thou new Pentecosts, swift with salvation,
   Fair spring the myrtle where once stood the thorn.

4 God speed the gospel! Enflame them that hear it,
   All men and us, to declare Thy glad reign.
   Conquer the world by the sword of Thy Spirit,
   Hasten Immanuel's coming again!

297 Soon may the last glad song arise.

L. M. *" For the sake of the Name they went forth."* **Missionary Chant.**
MRS. VOKES, 1797. *Abr.* HEINRICH C. ZEUNER, 1832.

1 SOON may the last glad song arise
   Thro all the millions of the skies,
   That song of triumph which records
   That all the Earth is now the Lord's!

2 Let thrones and powers and kingdoms be
   Obedient, mighty God, to Thee!
   And, over land and stream and main,
   Wave Thou the sceptre of Thy reign!

298 O Spirit of the living God!

L. M.   *" When they had prayed the place was shaken."*   **Rockingham.**

JAMES MONTGOMERY, 1825. *Abr.*   LOWELL MASON, 1830.

1. O Spir-it of the liv-ing God! In all Thy plen-i-tude of grace,

Wher-e'er the foot of man hath trod, De-scend on our a-pos-tate race.

299

2 Give tongues of fire, and hearts of love,
To preach the reconciling Word.
Give power and unction from above,
Whene'er the joyful sound is heard.

3 Be darkness, at Thy coming, light!
Confusion—order, in Thy path.
Souls without strength inspire with might,
Bid mercy triumph over wrath.

4 O Spirit of the Lord, prepare
All the round Earth her God to meet!
Breathe Thou abroad like morning air,
Till hearts of stone begin to beat.

5 Baptize the nations, far and nigh,
The triumphs of the Cross record.
The Name of Jesus glorify,
Till every kindred call Him Lord.

1 Go, LABOR on. Spend and be spent,
Thy joy to do the Father's will;
It is the way the Master went,
Should not the servant tread it still?

2 Go, labor on; 'tis not for naught;
Thine earthly loss is heavenly gain.
Men heed thee, love thee, praise thee not:
The Master praises,—what are men?

3 Go, labor on; enough, while here,
If He shall praise thee, if He deign
Thy willing heart to mark and cheer;
No toil for Him shall be in vain.

4 Toil on, and in thy toil rejoice;
For toil comes rest, for exile home.
Soon shalt thou hear the Bridegroom's voice,
The midnight peal: *"Behold I come!"*

HORATIUS BONAR, 1857. *Abr.*

Missions.

300   Eternal Father! Thou hast said.

L. M.   *" Now therefore be wise, O ye kings ! Be instructed ye judges of the Earth."*   **Park Street.**

RAY PALMER, 1860.   FREDERICO MARC A. VENUA, 1810.

Moto.

1. E - TER-NAL Fa - ther! Thou hast said, That Christ all glo - ry shall ob - tain, That He who

once a sufferer bled, Shall o'er the world, a conq'ror, reign, Shall o'er the world a conq'ror, reign.

2 We wait Thy triumph, Saviour King!
   Long ages have prepared Thy way;
   Now all abroad Thy banner fling,
   Set Time's great battle in array.

3 On mountain-tops the watch-fires glow,
   Where scattered wide the watchmen
     stand.

Voice echoes voice, and onward flow
   The joyous shouts, from land to land.

4 Oh, fill Thy Church with faith and power!
   Bid her long night of weeping cease.
   To groaning nations haste the hour,
   Of life and freedom, light and peace.

301   Our Father, Which art in Heaven.

Chant.   *" Peace upon the Israel of God."*   **Pater Noster.**

MATTHEW, VI: 9, 10.   GEORGE A. MACFARREN.

Our Father, Which...... | art | in | Heaven | Hal- | low - ed | be | Thy | Name.
The kingdom come. Thy | will | be | done | In | Earth as it | is | in | Heaven.

302 Saviour! sprinkle many nations.

"And this gospel of the kingdom shall be preached in the whole world for a testimony unto all the nations; and then shall the end come."

8s & 7s, D.

ARTHUR CLEVELAND COXE, 1851.

The Austrian Hymn.

FRANZ JOSEPH HAYDN, 1797.

1. { Saviour! sprinkle many nations, Fruitful let Thy sorrows be. }
   { By Thy pains and conso-la-tions, Draw the Gentiles unto Thee. } Of Thy Cross the wondrous story,

Be it to the na-tions told, Let them see Thee in Thy glory And Thy mer-cy man-i - fold.

2 Far and wide, to all unknowing,
   Pants for Thee each mortal breast.
   Human tears for Thee are flowing,
   Human hearts in Thee would rest.
   Thirsting, as for dews of even,
   As the new-mown grass for rain,
   Thee they seek, as God of Heaven,
   Thee, as Man, for sinners slain.

3 Saviour, lo! the isles are waiting,
   Stretched the hand, and strained the
   For Thy Spirit, new creating,   [sight,
   Love's pure flame and wisdom's light.
   Give the word, and of the preacher
   Speed the foot, and touch the tongue,
   Till on Earth, by every creature,
   Glory to the Lamb be sung!

303

1 FROM thy broad Atlantic harbors,
   Where the thronging thousands wait,
   To the West, whose sunset glories
   Flood Pacific's "Golden Gate",
   O'er our blooming plains and prairies,
   O'er these mountain summits grand,
   Every breeze the message carries,—
   "This shall be Immanuel's land!"

2 In thy heritage rejoicing,
   Guard, O Land, thy sacred trust.
   Faithful to thy glorious mission,
   Win the blessings of the just;
   Thro thy spreading towns and hamlets,
   Shed the light of truth divine.
   Over forest glade and bayou,
   Let its kindling radiance shine.

Missions.

304

3 God of Nations! our Defender
  In the paths of peril trod,
  Thro the centuries our Leader,
  Guide us still, our father's God!
  Lead the nation, Holy Spirit,
  Down the ages, strong and free!
  Lead, till Shiloh lift His banner,
  And to Him the gathering be!
                              ANON.

WE are living, we are dwelling,
  In a grand and awful time,
  In an age on ages telling,—
  To be living is sublime!
  Worlds are charging, Heaven beholding;
  Thou hast but an hour to fight;
  Now the blazoned Cross unfolding,
  On—right onward, for the right!
                    ARTHUR C. COXE, 1840. Abr.

305   God of the nations! bow Thine ear.

" Having hope that as your faith groweth we shall be magnified in you, so as to preach the gospel even unto the parts beyond you."

8.8.6.8.8.6.

(ALL VOICES IN UNISON.)

THOMAS HASTINGS, 1834. Abr.

Aithlone.

HEINRICH ISAAC, 1490.
Har. JOHANN SEB. BACH, d. 1750.

1. God of the na-tions! bow Thine ear, And listen to our fervent pray'r, Thro Thy be-lov-ed Son.

marcato.

Build up the kingdom of His grace, A - mid the mill-ions of our race, And make Thy wonders known.

2 Oh! let the nations rise, and bring
  Their offerings to th'almighty King,
  And trust in Him alone,
  Renounce their idols, and adore
  The God of gods for evermore,
  Upon His holy throne.

306   Father, let Thy kingdom come!

7.7.7.7.   *" The day I bid you shout, then shall ye shout."*   **Posen.**

JOHN PAGE HOPPS, 1877.   GEORG CHRISTOPH STRATTNER, 1691.

1. FATHER, let Thy kingdom come! Let it come with living power. Speak at length the fin-al word, Ush-er in the tri-umph hour.

2 As it came in days of old,
In the deepest hearts of men,
When Thy martyrs died for Thee,
Let it come, O God, again.

3 Tyrant thrones and idol shrines,
Let them from their place be hurled.
Enter on Thy better reign,
Wear the crown of this poor world.

4 Oh, what long, sad years have gone,
Since Thy Church was taught this prayer!

Oh, what eyes have watched and wept
For the dawning everywhere!

5 Break, triumphant day of God!
Break at last, our hearts to cheer;
Eager souls and earnest songs
Wait to hail Thy dawning here.

6 Empires, temples, sceptres, thrones,—
May they all for God be won!
And on earth made one with Heaven,
Father, may Thy will be done.

307   God of mercy, God of grace.

7.7.7.   *" Let all the peoples praise Thee."*   **Vienna.**

HENRY F. LYTE, 1834. *Abr. Arr.*   J. HEINRICH KNECHT, 1795.

1. GOD of mer-cy, God of grace, Show the brightness of Thy face, Shine up-on us, Sav-iour, shine,

Missions.

Fill Thy Church with light di - vine.

2 Let the people praise Thee, Lord,
Let Thy love on all be poured,
And Thy saving health extend
Unto Earth's remotest end.

3 Let the nations shout and sing
Glory to their Saviour King,
At Thy feet their tribute pay,
And Thy holy will obey.

308   The Lord will come and not be slow.

C. M.   *" He walketh on the vault of Heaven."*   **Dunfermline.**

JOHN MILTON, 1648. *Abr.*   SCOTCH PSALTER, 1615.

1. THE Lord will come and not be slow, His foot - steps can - not err;

Be - fore Him right - eous - ness shall go, His roy - al har - bin - ger.

2 Truth from the Earth, a beauteous flower,
Shall bud and blossom then;
And Justice, from her heavenly bower,
Look down on mortal men.

3 Rise, Lord, judge Thou the Earth in might,
This longing Earth redress;
For Thou art He who shall by right
· The nations all possess.

4 The nations all whom Thou hast made
Shall come, and all shall frame
To bow them low before Thee, Lord,
And glorify Thy name.

5 For great Thou art, and wonders great
By Thy strong hand are done;
Thou, in Thine everlasting seat,
Remainest God alone.

Missions.

309 From Greenland's icy mountains.

"Giving them the Holy Ghost even as He did unto us."

7s & 6s, D.
Reginald Heber, 1819. Abr.

Missionary Hymn.
Lowell Mason, 1823.

1. From Greenland's i - cy mountains, From In - dia's cor - al strand, Where Afric's sun-ny fount - ains Roll down their gold - en sand,— From many an an - cient riv - er, From many a palm - y plain, They call us to de - liv - er Their land from error's chain.

2 Can we, whose souls are lighted
   With wisdom from on high,
Can we, to men benighted,
   The lamp of life deny?
Salvation, oh! salvation!
   The joyful sound proclaim,
Till each remotest nation
   Hath learned Messiah's name.

3 Waft, waft, ye winds! His story,
   And ye, ye waters! roll,
Till, like a sea of glory,
   It spreads from pole to pole,
Till, o'er our ransomed nature,
   The Lamb for sinners slain,
Redeemer, King, Creator,
   In bliss returns to reign!

310   When wilt Thou save the people?

" He was moved with compassion for them ; because they were distressed and scattered."

7s, 6s ; 8s & 5. P.   **Commonwealth.**

EBENEZER ELLIOTT, 1831.   JOSIAH BOOTH, 1888.

1. WHEN wilt Thou save the peo - ple? O God of mer-cy, when? Not kings and lords: but na - tions! Not thrones and crowns: but men! Flowers of Thy heart, O God, are they; Let them not pass, like weeds a - way, Their her - i - tage a sun - less day. GOD SAVE THE PEO - PLE!

2 Shall crime bring crime for ever,
  Strength aiding still the strong?
Is it Thy will, O Father,
  That man shall toil for wrong?
No! say Thy mountains, *No!* Thy skies;
Man's clouded sun shall brightly rise,
And songs ascend instead of sighs.
  GOD SAVE THE PEOPLE!

3 When wilt Thou save the people?
  O God of mercy, when?
The people, Lord, the people,
  Not thrones and crowns: but men!
God save the people; let them share
Childhood and love with angels fair;
From sin and bondage and despair,
  GOD SAVE THE PEOPLE!

311 To Thee, our God, we fly.

6.6.6.6.8.8. *"That thou mayest fear this glorious and fearful name, THE LORD THY GOD."* **Dudley.**

WILLIAM W. HOW, 1871. Abr.   EDWARD F. RIMBAULT, 1867.

1. To THEE, our God, we fly, For mer-cy and for grace. Oh hear our low-ly cry, And hide not

Thou Thy face. O Lord, stretch forth Thy mighty hand, And guard and bless our Fath - er - land.

2 Arise, O Lord of Hosts!
  Be jealous for Thy Name,
  And drive from out our coasts
  The sins that put to shame.
  O Lord, stretch forth Thy, etc.

3 The powers ordained by Thee
  With heavenly wisdom bless,
  May they Thy servants be,
  And rule in righteousness.
  O Lord, stretch forth Thy, etc.

312 My Country! 'tis of thee.

6s & 4s.   *"A nation and a company of nations shall be of thee."*   **America.**

SAMUEL F. SMITH, 1832.   *Adapta of* HENRY CAREY, 1740.

1. My COUNTRY! 'tis of thee, Sweet land of lib - er - ty, Of thee I sing; Land where my

National.

fathers died! Land of the pilgrims' pride! From ev - ery mount-ain side Let freedom ring.

2 My native country, thee,
Land of the noble, free,
Thy name I love.
I love thy rocks and rills,
Thy woods and templed hills,
My heart with rapture thrills
Like that above.

3 Let music swell the breeze,
And ring from all the trees
Sweet freedom's song.

Let mortal tongues awake,
Let all that breathe partake,
Let rocks their silence break,
The sound prolong.

4 Our fathers' God, to Thee,
Author of liberty,
To Thee we sing!
Long may our land be bright
With freedom's holy light;
Protect us by Thy might,
Great God, our King.

---

313   ## Now thank we all our God.

"He hath not dealt with us after our sins."

6.7.6.7.6.6.6.6.

Ger. MARTIN RINKART, 1644.
Tr. CATH. WINKWORTH, 1858.

"Nun Danket alle Gott."

JOHANN CRUGER, 1648.

1. { Now THANK we all our God, With hearts and hands and voic - es, }
{ Who wondrous things hath done, In Whom His world re - joic - es. } Who from our moth-er's

arms Hath blest us on our way With countless gifts of love, And still is ours to - day.

314 God the All-terrible King, who ordainest.

" When Thy judgments are in the Earth, the inhabitants of the world learn righteousness."

11.10.11.9.
HENRY F. CHORLEY, 1854. *Abr.*

Russian Hymn.
ALEXIS LVOFF, 1833. *Har.* by H. P. MAIN.

1. GOD the All-ter-ri-ble King, who or-dain-est Great winds Thy cla-rions, the lightnings Thy sword,

Show forth Thy pit - y on high where Thou reign-est! Give to us peace in our time, O Lord.

2 God the Omnipotent, mighty Avenger,
   Watching invisible, judging unheard,
   Doom us not now in the hour of our danger:
   Give to us peace in our time, O Lord.

3 God the All merciful! Earth hath forsaken
   Thy ways of blessedness, slighted Thy word;
   Bid not Thy wrath in its terrors awaken!
   Give to us peace in our time, O Lord.

4 God the All-righteous One! man hath defied Thee;
   Yet to eternity standeth Thy word;
   Falsehood and wrong shall not tarry beside Thee;
   Give to us peace in our time, O Lord!

5 God the All-wise! by the fire of Thy chastening,
   Earth shall to freedom and truth be restored.
   Thro the thick darkness Thy kingdom is hastening;
   Thou wilt give peace in Thy time, O Lord!

315 God save our land!

10.12.10.4. " *Grace, grace unto it.* " **Virginia.**
M. W. S., 1881. CONRAD KOCHER, 1844.
Vigoroso.

1. GOD SAVE OUR LAND! Be this our steadfast pray'r; Thy king-dom come with pow'r and glo - ry

ff lento.

ev - ery-where: Let all our souls in - voke Thine aw - ful care:— *God save our land!*

2 Keep Thou our flag! Avert unholy wars,
  Let tears of godly sorrow cleanse each stain that mars,
  Thro stripes lead upward to the bright'ning stars. *God save our land!*

3 "In God we trust!" O Lord, Thine arm make bare,
  By Thy pure word smite pride, hate, lust and lies that dare,
  Nor let Thy faithful rod our evil spare. *God save our land!*

4 Guide them that rule! Our blood-bought freedom keep.
  Let union, love, and law, their happy harvest reap,
  Till in thanksgiving deep shall answer deep. *God save our land!*

5 Full with Thy blessing, counselled 'neath Thine eye,
  Who ridest for our help upon the bending sky;—
  What nation is there which hath God so nigh? *God save our land!*

6 Let Jesus reign! and every heart consent.
  Of Him, by Him, for Him, be all the government.
  Sign with His Cross a ransomed continent. GOD SAVE OUR LAND!

A - - MEN.

316
Thank thy God forever.

6s & 5s.
M. W. S., 1892.

"Turn ye not aside after vain things that cannot profit."
(VOICES IN UNISON.)

Ezekiel.
ARTHUR S. SULLIVAN, 1872.

1. THANK thy God for-ev - er, O thou land of choice, Praise Him as His peo - ple With a mighty voice!

In His name we tri-umph, Holy, wise and just. He up-holds our ban-ners. In our God we trust.

f Refrain.

Thank thy God for-ev - er, O thou land of choice, Praise Him as His peo-ple With a might-y voice!

2 Son of Man, Thy covenant
Makes the nation free;
Only Thy dominion
Is our liberty.
Set Thy cross, O Saviour,
O'er our starry sky;
By that sign we conquer,
Lift it up on high!
Thank Thy God, etc.

3 Move upon the waters,
O Thou Living Breath!
Once again Thy mandate
Change the waste of death.
End the time-long torment
Of Earth's wrong and pain,
Bind her broken kingdoms
'Neath Messiah's reign.
Thank Thy God, etc.

317   O God, beneath Thy guiding hand.

L. M.   *" The Lord our God be with us as He was with our fathers."*   **Incarnation.**

LEONARD BACON, 1838, 1844.   MARTIN LUTHER, 1535.

1. O God, be - neath Thy guid - ing hand, Our ex - iled fa - thers crost the sea,

And when they trod the win - try strand, With prayer and psalm they wor-shipt Thee.

2 Thou heard'st, well pleased, the song, the
pray'r:
Thy blessing came; and still its power
Shall onward, thro all ages, bear
The memory of that holy hour.

3 Laws, freedom, truth and faith in God,
Came with those exiles o'er the waves,
And where their pilgrim feet have trod,
The God they trusted guards their
graves.

4 And here Thy name, O God of love!
Their children's children shall adore,
Till these eternal hills remove,
And spring adorns the Earth no more.

318 God of our fathers.

9.9.9.9.
M. W. S., 1889. *Abr.*
Maestoso.

"The bow that is in the cloud in the day of rain."

Ithaca.
WILLIAM PIUTTI, 1864.

1. God of our fa-thers, our God to-day, Deep are Thy coun-sels, high is Thy hand!

Still for Thy guidance humb-ly we pray; Spare Thou the peo-ple, save Thou the land!

Copyright, 1888 and 1889, by Biglow & Main

2 Healer of nations! Life-giving God!
Purify, chasten, keep by Thy grace,
Show us Thy pardons, shatter Thy rod,
Gather and hold us in Thine embrace.

3 Stand Thou above us, Sun, Lord, and Shield!
March Thou before us, Pillar of Flame!
Earth then her increase gladly shall yield,
Yea, all her peoples shout to Thy name.

319 Now to heaven our prayer ascending.

8s & 4s, P.
W. E. HICKSON.

"In the name of our God will we set up our banners."

God Speed.
German.

1. Now to Heav'n our pray'r ascending, God speed the right; In a no-ble cause contending, God speed the right.

Seasons.

Be our zeal in Heav'n recorded, With success on Earth rewarded, GOD SPEED THE RIGHT, GOD SPEED THE RIGHT.

2 Be that prayer again repeated,
  God speed the right;
  Ne'er despairing, tho defeated,
  God speed the right;
  Like the good and great in story,
  If we fail, we fail with glory.

3 Patient, firm and persevering,
  God speed the right;
  Ne'er th' event nor danger fearing,
  God speed the right.
  Pain nor toil nor trial heeding,
  In the strength of Heaven succeeding.

320   Break, new-born year.

C. M.   *"If the Lord will, we shall both live and do this or that."*   Eloise.

THOMAS HORNBLOWER GILL., 1853.   HUBERT P. MAIN, 1874.

1. BREAK, new-born year, on glad eyes break! Me - lo - dious voic - es move!

On, roll - ing Time! thou canst not make The Fa - ther cease to love.

2 The parted year had wingèd feet:
  The Saviour still doth stay.
  The New Year comes: but, Spirit sweet,
  Thou goest not away.

3 Lord! from this year more service win,
  More glory, more delight!
  Oh make its hours less sad with sin,
  Its days with Thee more bright!

321   Come let us, anew, our journey pursue.

5s & 11s. P.   *"If the Lord will, we shall both live and do this or that."*   **Weimar.**
CHARLES WESLEY, 1749. *Alt.*   WILLIAM PIUTTI, 1883.

1. COME let us, a - new, our journey pur-sue, Roll round with the year And never stand still till the Mas-ter ap-pear; His a - dor - a - ble will let us glad-ly ful - fill, and our tal-ents im - prove By the patience of hope, and the la-bor of love,— By the patience of hope, and the la-bor of love.

2 Our life is a dream, our time, as a stream, glides swiftly away;
    The fugitive moment refuses to stay.
  Lo, the arrow is flown! and the moment is gone. The millenial year
    Rushes on to our view, and eternity's near.

3 Oh, that each, in that day of advent, may say, "I've fought my way thro;
    I've finished the work Thou didst give me to do."
  Oh, that each, from his Lord, may receive the glad word, "Well and faith-
        fully done!
  Enter into My joy, and sit down on My throne!"

Seasons.

322   Father, let me dedicate all this year.

7s & 5s, D.   *" In nothing be anxious."*   **Salome.**

LAWRENCE TUTTIETT, 1863.   GEORGE A. MACFARREN, 1881.

1. FA - THER, let me ded - i - cate All this year to Thee, In what - ev - er

world - ly state Thou wilt have me be: Not from sor - row, pain, or care

Free - dom dare I claim; This a - lone shall be my pray'r,—"Glo - ri - fy Thy Name."

2 Can a child presume to choose
    Where or how to live?
Can a Father's love refuse
    All the best to give?
More Thou givest every day
    Than the best can claim,
Nor withholdest aught that may
    Glorify Thy Name.

3 If in mercy Thou wilt spare
    Joys that yet are mine;
If on life, serene and fair,
    Brighter rays may shine;
Let my glad heart, while it sings,
    Thee in all proclaim,
And, whate'er the future brings,
    Glorify Thy Name.

323   Ring out the old, ring in the new.

L. M.   *" In that day shall there be upon the bells—HOLY UNTO THE LORD!"*   **Mainzer.**

ALFRED TENNYSON, 1850. *Abr.*   JOSEPH MAINZER, 1841.

1. Ring out the old, ring in the new, Ring, hap-py bells, a-cross the snow:

The year is go-ing, let him go; Ring out the false, ring in the true.

2 Ring out the grief that saps the mind
  For those that here we see no more;
  Ring out the feud of rich and poor,
  Ring in redress to all mankind.

3 Ring out false pride in place and blood,
  The civic slander and the spite;
  Ring in the love of truth and right,
  Ring in the common love of good.

4 Ring out old shapes of foul disease,
  Ring out the narrowing lust of gold;
  Ring out the thousand wars of old,
  Ring in the thousand years of peace.

5 Ring in the valiant man and free,
  The larger heart, the kindlier hand;
  Ring out the darkness of the land;
  Ring in the Christ that is to be!

324   Our Helper, God, we bless Thy name.

L. M.   *" I will walk at liberty; for I have sought Thy precepts."*   **Statham.**

PHILIP DODDRIDGE, 1755. *Abr.*   FRANCIS R. STATHAM, 1872.

1. Our Help-er, God, we bless Thy name, Whose love for-ev-er is the same;

The tok-ens of Thy gra-cious care Be - gin and crown and close the year.

2 Thus far Thine arm hath led us on:
Thus far we make Thy mercy known;
And while we tread this desert land,
New mercies shall new songs demand.

3 Our grateful souls on Jordan's shore
Shall raise one sacred pillar more,
Then bear, in Thy bright courts above,
Inscriptions of immortal love.

325   The flowers that bloom in sun and shade.

8.6.4.8.6.4.   *"And we shall be changed."*   Cayuga.

CHRISTINA G. ROSSETTI, 1878.   MAX PIUTTI, 1883.

Adagio.

1. THE flowers that bloom in sun and shade, And glit - ter in the dew, The flowers must fade.

The birds that build their nest and sing, When love-ly spring is new, Must soon take wing.

2 The Sun that rises in His strength,
To wake and warm the world,
    Must set at length.
The sea that overflows the shore,
    With billows frothed and curled,
    Must ebb once more.

3 All come and go, all wax and wane,
    O Lord, save only Thou,
    Who dost remain
The same to all eternity;
    All things which fail us now
    We trust to Thee.

326   Summer suns are glowing.

6s & 5s, D.   *"The first Author of Beauty hath created them."*   **Ruth.**

WILLIAM WALSHAM HOW, 1871. *Abr.*   SAMUEL SMITH, 1871.

1. SUMMER suns are glow-ing Ov - er land and sea. Happy light is flow-ing, Boun - ti - ful and free.

Ev-'ry-thing re - joic - es, In the mellow rays. Earth's ten thousand voic-es Swell the psalm of praise.

2 God's free mercy streameth
Over all the world,
And His banner gleameth,
Everywhere unfurled.
Broad and deep and glorious,
As the heaven above,
Shines in might victorious
His eternal love.

3 We will never doubt Thee,
Tho Thou veil Thy light.
Life is dark without Thee,
Death with Thee is bright.
Light of light, shine o'er us
On our pilgrim way,
Go Thou still before us
To the endless day.

327   The year is swiftly waning.

"Reaping their wheat harvest in the valley, they lifted up their eyes, and saw the ark and rejoiced."

7.6.7.6.   **"Christus, mein Leben."**

WILLIAM WALSHAM HOW, 1871. *Abr.*   MELCHOIR VULPIUS, 1609.

1. THE year is swift-ly wan - ing; The sum - mer days are past; And life, brief life, is

Seasons.

speed - ing; The end is nearing fast.

2 The ever-changing seasons
   In silence come and go :
   But Thou, Eternal Father,
   No time nor change canst know.

3 Behold the bending orchards
   With bounteous fruit are crowned ;
   Lord, in our hearts more richly
   Let heavenly fruits abound.

328   Sing to the Lord of harvest!

7s & 6s, D.   *"It is He that giveth thee power to get wealth."*   **St. Theodulph.**

JOHN S. B. MONSELL, 1862. *Abr.*   MELCHOIR TESCHNER, 1613.

1. { Sing to the Lord of har-vest ! Sing songs of love and praise ! }
   { With joy-ful hearts and voic - es Your al - le - lu - ias raise. } By Him the roll-ing sea-sons In

fruit - ful or - der move; Sing to the Lord of har - vest A song of hap-py love.

2 By Him the clouds drop fatness
   The deserts bloom and spring,
   The hills leap up in gladness,
   The valleys laugh and sing.
   He filleth with His fullness
   All things with large increase,
   He crowns the year with goodness,
   With plenty and with peace.

3 Heap on His sacred altar
   The gifts His goodness gave,
   The golden sheaves of harvest,
   The souls He died to save.
   Your hearts lay down before Him
   When at His feet ye fall,
   And with your lives adore Him
   Who gave His life for all !

329 Come, ye thankful people.

" Your threshing shall reach unto your vintage, and the vintage shall reach unto the sowing time, and ye shall eat your bread to the full."

7s, D.

Henry Alford, 1844 *Abr.*

St. George's.

George Job Elvey, 1859.

1. Come, ye thank-ful peo-ple, come, Raise the song of Har-vest-home; All is safe-ly gath-er'd in, Ere the win-ter storms be-gin. God, our Mak-er, doth pro-vide For our wants to be supplied Come to God's own temple, come, Raise the song of Harvest-home.

2 All the world is God's own field,
Fruit unto His praise to yield;
Wheat and tares together sown,
Unto joy or sorrow grown;
First the blade, and then the ear,
Then the full corn shall appear.
Lord of Harvest, grant that we
Wholesome grain and pure may be.

3 Even so, Lord, quickly come
To Thy final Harvest-home.
Gather Thou Thy people in,
Free from sorrow, free from sin;
There for ever purified,
In Thy presence to abide.
Come with all Thine angels, come,
Raise the glorious Harvest-home.

330   Harsh and dread the Winter reigns.

7.7.7.7.8.8.   *" He sendeth forth His snow like wool."*   **Christlight.**

M. W. S., 1896.   JOSEPH BARNBY, 1874.

1. Harsh and dread the Win - ter reigns, Smit-ing with his i - cy hand Pris-oned streams and shroud-ed plains; Bare and gaunt the for - ests stand: But the Earth is on - ly sleep-ing, Life its treasure safe is keep - ing.

Years are hurrying to their last:
But a Spring-tide sure is breaking,
Resurrection life partaking.

2 Thrush and blue-bird choirs are still,
    Blithesome ways are lone and drear,
Moaning winds o'er hurst and hill
Wail the requiem of the year:
But His loving wisdom keepeth,
Once who said—"She only sleepeth."

3 Faded leaf and fallen bloom,
    So our days are briefly past,
Cometh age with cold and gloom,

4 He who with the Winter's fleece
    Shelters warm each root and germ,
Shall our slumberings guard in peace,—
All Earth's parable confirm;
Death and darkness cannot hold us,
So His changeless power enfold us.

5 Restless seasons, storm and shine,
    Glittering frost and summer glow,
Starlight, daylight,—He is mine,
There above and here below!
June shall follow all December;
Love and Life will aye remember.

Seasons.

331 Watch, brethren, watch! The year is dying.

9.9.8.8.8.8.   *"The night is far spent,"*   **Tryst.**

Horatius Bonar.   Robert Lowry, 1884.

1. Watch, brethren, watch! The year is dy-ing. Watch, brethren, watch! Old Time is fly-ing.

Watch, as ye watch the part-ing breath, And as ye watch for life, or death;

marcato.

E - ter - ni - ty is draw-ing nigh! E - ter - ni - ty! E - ter - ni - ty!

Copyright, 1884, by Biglow & Main

2 Pray, brethren, pray! The sands are falling.
Pray, brethren, pray! God's voice is calling.
You turret strikes the dying chime.
We kneel upon the edge of time. *Eternity is, etc.*

3 Praise, brethren, praise! The skies are rending.
Praise, brethren, praise! The fight is ending.
Oh see, the glory cometh near!
The King Himself will soon be here! *Eternity is, etc.*

Immortality.

332   One sweetly solemn thought.

S. M.   *"Now is salvation nearer to us than when we first believed."*   **Newland.**

PHŒBE CARY 1852. *Abr. Alt.*   HENRY JOHN GAUNTLETT, 1857.

1. ONE sweet-ly sol-emn thought Comes to me o'er and o'er, That I am near-er
2. Near-er my Fa-thers house, Where ma-ny mansions be; Near-er the great white

home to day, Than e'er I've been be-fore!
judgment-throne, Nearer the crys-tal sea.

3 Nearer the bound where life
    May lay its burden down,
And leave its cross of heavy grief
    To gain the starry crown.

4 Nearer that silent stream,
    Down winding thro the night,
Beyond whose swelling waters gleam
    The coasts of perfect light!

333   For me to live is Christ.

S. M.   *"Consider the Apostle and High Priest of our confession."*   **Rialto.**

ANON, 1859. *Abr.*   GEORGE F. ROOT, 1859.

1. FOR me to live is Christ, To die is endless gain; For Him I gladly bear the cross, And welcome grief and pain.

2 I fare with Christ my Lord;
    His path the path I choose ;
They joy who suffer most with Him—
    They win who with Him lose.

3 The dawn on distant hills
    Shines o'er the vales below.

The shadows of this world are lost
    In light to which I go.

4 Faithful may I endure,
    And hear my Saviour say,
Thrice welcome home, belovéd child
    Inherit endless day !

Immortality.

334 Come, Lord, when grace hath made me meet.

C. M.   *"That where I am there ye may be."*   **Wiltshire.**

RICHARD BAXTER, 1681. *Abr.*   GEORGE THOMAS SMART, 1800.

1 COME, Lord, when grace hath made me
   Thy blessèd face to see;   [meet,
For if Thy work on Earth be sweet,
   What will Thy glory be!

2 My knowledge of that life is small,
   The eye of faith is dim:
But 'tis enough that Christ knows all
   And I shall be with Him.

335   Asleep in Jesus! blessèd sleep!

L. M.   **Harborlight.**

MARGARET MACKAY, 1832. *Abr.*   HUBERT P. MAIN, 1889.

1. A-SLEEP in Je - sus! blessèd sleep! From which none ever wakes to weep! A calm and

un-dis-turbed re - pose, A calm and un-dis-turbed re - pose Un-brok-en by the last of foes!

Immortality.

2 Asleep in Jesus! peaceful rest,
Whose waking is supremely blest;
No fear, no woe, shall dim that hour
That manifests the Saviour's power.

3 Asleep in Jesus! far from thee
Thy kindred and their graves may be:
But thine is still a blessèd sleep,
From which none ever wakes to weep.

336   There the wicked cease from troubling.

Fugue.   *"I know that my Avenger liveth."*   **Requiem.**

JOB, III: 17   W. A. MOZART, 1791.

There the wick - ed cease from troub-ling, and the
There the wick - ed cease from troub-ling,

There the wick - ed cease from troub-ling, and the
There the wick - ed cease from troub-ling, and the wea - ry

Instrument.

wea - ry, and the wea - ry be .... at rest.   A - - - - - men.
and the wea - ry, and the wea - ry be .... at rest.   A - - - - - men.
be ....

wea - ry and the wea - ry be .... at rest.   A - - - - men.
and the wea - ry be .... at rest.   A - - - - men.

Immortality.

337　When my last hour is close at hand.

8.7.8.7.8.8.7.　　　"*Every morning doth He bring His judgment to light.*"　　**Luther's Hymn.**
Ger. NICOLAUS HERMAN, 1562.　　　　　　　　　　　　　　　　JOSEPH KLUG'S GESANGBUCH, 1535.
Tr. EDGAR ALFRED BOWRING, 1861. *Abr.*

1. { When my last hour is close at hand. My last sad jour-ney tak-en } O Lord, my spir-it
   { Do Thou, Lord Je-sus, by me stand, Let me not be for-sak-en. }

I re-sign In-to Thy lov-ing hands di-vine; 'Tis safe with-in Thy keep-ing.

2 And so to Jesus Christ I'll go,
　　My longing arms extending;
　　So fall asleep, in slumber deep,
　　Slumber that knows no ending,
　　Till Jesus Christ, God's only Son,
　　Op'ning the gates of bliss, leads on
　　To Heaven,—to life eternal.

338　Gently, Lord, oh gently lead us.

8s & 7s. D.　　　　　"*Certainly I will be with thee.*"　　　　**Harmony.**
THOMAS HASTINGS, 1831, 1850.　　　　　　　　　　GEORGE F. HANDEL, 1721. *Arr.*

1. { Gently, Lord, oh gen-tly lead us, Pil-grims in this vale of tears, } When temptation's darts assail us,
   { Thro the tri-als yet de-creed us, Till our last great change appear. }

Immortality.

When in devious paths we stray, Let Thy goodness nev-er fail us, Lead us in Thy per-fect way.

2 In the hour of pain and anguish,
   In the hour when death draws near,
   Suffer not our hearts to languish,
   Suffer not our souls to fear;

And, when mortal life is ended,
Bid us in Thine arms to rest,
Till, by angel bands attended,
We awake among the blest.

339 Tranquilly, slowly, solemnly, lowly.

5.5.9.5.5.9.   *"That, whether we wake or sleep, we should live together with Him."*   Urijah.

M. W. S., 1884. *Abr.*   CARL HEINRICH GRAUN, d. 1759. *Arr.*

Marche funebre.

1. TRANQUILLY, slow-ly, Sol-emn-ly, low-ly, Bring the precious earth that sleep hath kissed!

Soul to its Mak-er, Dust to God's a - cre, Qui - et bid - ing res-ur-rec-tion tryst.

2 With eyes bedimming,
   Requiems hymning,
Smite we music from these broken chords;
   Yet smile in grieving,
   Calmly believing,
Tho we live or die, we are the Lord's.

3 Loosed Earth's last fetter!
   Sure 'tis far better
To depart and be for aye with Christ;
   So come, Lord Jesus,
   Soon to release us,
Join us with the souls emparadised!

340   Earth, with its dark and dreadful ills.

C. M.   "*All live unto Him.*"   **Anastasia.**

ALICE CARY, 1870.   LUDWIG VAN BEETHOVEN, 1791.

1. EARTH, with its dark and dread - ful ills, Re - cedes, and fades a - way;

Lift up your heads, ye heaven - ly hills, Ye gates of death, give - way!

2 My soul is full of whispered song,
  My blindness is my sight,
The shadows that I feared so long
Are all alive with light.

3 The while my pulses faintly beat,
  My faith doth so abound
I feel grow firm beneath my feet
The fair immortal ground.

4 That faith to me a courage gives
  Low as the grave to go:
I know that my Redeemer lives;
That I shall live, I know.

5 The palace walls I almost see,
  Where dwells my Lord and King;
O death, where is thy victory?
O death, where is thy sting?

341

1 LIGHT of the lonely pilgrim's heart!
  Star of the coming day!
Arise, and with Thy morning beams
Chase all our griefs away.

2 Come, blessèd Lord! let every shore
  And answering island sing
The praises of Thy royal name,
And own Thee as their King,

3 Bid the whole Earth, responsive now
  To the bright world above,
Break forth in sweetest strains of joy
In memory of Thy love.

4 Thine was the Cross, with all its fruits
  Of grace and peace divine;
Be Thine the crown of glory now,
The palm of victory Thine.

EDWARD DENNY, 1842. *Abr.*

342   A voice is heard on Earth of kinsfolk weeping.

Chant.   *" Behold I die : but God shall be with you."*   **Whittier.**

James D. Burns, 1854. *Abr.*   *Arr.* M. W. S., 1883.

Piano.

1. A voice is heard on *Earth* of . . . . kins - folk weeping   The *loss* of   one   they   love;

rit.

But he is gone where *the* re - - - - deemed are   keeping   Their   festi - val a - bove.

Copyright, 1885, by Biglow & Main.

2 The mourners throng the *way*, and | from the | steeple |
   The funer*al* | bell tolls | slow : ||
   But on the golden *streets* the | holy | people |
   Are *passing* | to and | fro, ||

3 And saying as they *meet*, 'Re- | joice! an- | other, |
   Long *waited* | for, is | come.' ||
   The Saviour's heart is *glad*; a | younger | brother |
   Hath reached the | Father's | home. ||

343

1 Sunset and | evening | star, | And one *clear* | call for | me! ||
   And may there *be* no | moaning ' of the | bar | When I *put* | out to | sea. ||

2 But such a tide as *moving* | seems a- | sleep, | Too *full* for | sound and | foam, ||
   When that which drew from *out* the | boundless | deep, | *Turns* | again | home. ||

3 *Twilight* and | evening | bell, | And *af*ter | that the | dark! ||
   And may there be no *sadness* | of fare- | well, | *When* | I em- | bark. ||

4 For tho from out our *bourne* of | Time and | Place, | The *flood* may | bear me | far, |'
   I hope to see my *Pi*lot | face to | face | When I *have* | crost the | bar. ||

                                   Alfred Tennyson, 1889.

344　O Paradise! Who doth not crave for rest?

8s & 6s, P.　　　*" Where is the way to the dwelling of light."*　　　**Paradise.**

FREDERICK W. FABER, 1854. *Abr.*　　　HENRY SMART, 1868.

1. O Par - a - dise! O Par - a - dise! Who doth not crave for rest? Who would not seek the hap - py land Where they that loved are blest? Where loy - al hearts and true Stand ev - er in the light, All rap - ture thro and thro, In God's most ho - ly sight. A - men.

2 O Paradise! O Paradise!
　The world is growing old;
Who would not be at rest and free
Where love is never cold?
　Where loyal hearts, etc.

3 O Paradise! O Paradise!
　'Tis weary waiting here;
I long to be where Jesus is,
To feel, to see Him near;
　Where loyal hearts, etc.

4 O Paradise! O Paradise!
　I want to sin no more,
I want to be as pure on Earth
As on thy spotless shore,
　Where loyal hearts, etc.

5 Lord Jesus, King of Paradise,
　Oh, keep us in Thy love,
And guide us to that happy land
Of perfect rest above.
　Where loyal hearts, etc.

345 The blessèd saints about Thee.

7s & 6s, D.   ... *Christ, who is our life, shall be manifested."*   **Gottland.**
HERVEY D. GANSE, 1887.   Swedish. LINDEMAN'S KORAL-BOK.

1. { THE blessèd saints a - bout Thee, O Christ, are pure and strong: }
{ We languish here without Thee, How long, O Lord, how long? } When shall the heavens be bending

Be-neath th' un-numbered wings, In ra - diant pomp at - tend - ing The com-ing King of kings?

2 No cross is now before Thee.
 There is no cross but one!
The blood-stained wood that bore Thee
 Outblazons now the Sun.
Such deathless splendors lighten
 Thy path in sorrow trod!—
What burst of Heaven shall brighten
 The coming of our God!

3 No earthly veil shall hide Thee,
 The Heavens no more withhold,
All glories pale beside Thee,
 Whom ranks of light infold.
Break thro the skies, and greet us
 From our eternal home!
Make haste, our Life, and meet us!
 Oh come, Lord Jesus, come!

346

1 AWAKE, awake, O Zion,
 Put on thy strength divine,
Thy garments bright in beauty,
 The bridal dress be thine!
Thine own Messiah cometh,
 Thy bridal day draws nigh,
The day of signs and wonders,
 And marvels from on high.

2 Break forth in hymns of gladness,
 O waste Jerusalem!
Let songs, instead of sadness,
 Thy jubilee proclaim!
The Lord shall build up Zion
 In glory and renown,
And Jesus, Judah's lion,
 Shall wear His rightful crown.

BENJAMIN GOUGH, 1865. *Arr.*

The Second Coming.

347 — All faded is the glowing light.

C. M.
THOMAS TOKE LYNCH, 1855.

" Why sayest thou? My way is hid from the Lord!"

Bernard.
BERTHOLD TOURS, 1866. Alt.

1. All fad-ed is the glow-ing light That once from Heav-en shone, When start-led shep-herds

in the night The an-gels came up - on.

2 Oh shine again, ye angel host,
  And say that He is near;
  Tho but a simple few at most
  Believe He will appear.

3 Ye Heavens, that have been growing dark,
  Now also are ye dumb;
  When shall the listeners say, "Hark!
  They're singing—He will come?"

4 Lord, come again, oh come again,
  Come even as Thou wilt;
  But not anew to suffer pain,
  And strive with human guilt.

5 Oh come again, Thou mighty King,
  Let Earth Thy glory see;
  And let us hear the angels sing,
  "He comes with victory."

348 — That day of wrath, that dreadful day.

L. M.
Lat. THOMAS OF CELANO, 1250. Abr.
Tr. WALTER SCOTT, 1805.

"In the morning the Lord will show who are His."

St. Cross.
JOHN B. DYKES, 1861.

1. That day of wrath, that dread - ful day, When Heav'n and Earth shall pass a - way!

The Second Coming.

What power shall be the sin - ner's stay? How shall He meet that dread - ful day?

2 When, shriveling like a parchèd scroll,
The flaming heavens together roll,
When louder yet, and yet more dread,
Swells the high trump that wakes the dead!

3 Oh, on that day, that wrathful day,
When man to judgment wakes from clay,
Be Thou the trembling sinner's stay!
Tho Heaven and Earth shall pass away.

349   O Son of God, in glory crowned.

" That we may have boldness in the day of judgment ; because as He is, even so are we in this world."

L. M.

CECIL F. ALEXANDER, 1853. *Abr.*

St. Jerome.

CARL HEINRICH GRAUN, 1720.

1. O Son of God, in glo-ry crowned, Thou Judge or-dain ed of quick and dead! O Son of Man, so

pit - ying found For all the tears Thy peo - ple shed! A - - - - men, A - men, A - men.

2 Lord, ere the last dread trump be heard,
And ere before Thy face we stand,
Look Thou on each accusing word,
And blot it with Thy bleeding hand!

3 And by the love that brought Thee here,
And by the Cross, and by the grave,
Give perfect love for conscious fear,
And in the day of judgment save! *Amen.*

350   Lo! He comes, with clouds descending.

"I am persuaded that He is able to guard that which I have committed unto Him against that day."

8s 7s, & 4.   Archangel.
CHARLES WESLEY, 1758. *Abr.*   MAX PIUTTI, 1880.

Maestoso.

1. Lo! He comes with clouds de - scend - ing, Once for fa - vored sin - ners slain.

Thousand thousand saints at - tend - ing, Swell the tri - umph of His train.

Al - - le - lu - - - ia! Je - sus comes, and comes to reign!

2 Every eye shall now behold Him,
    Robed in dreadful majesty.
  Those who set at naught and sold Him,
    Pierced, and nailed Him to the Tree,
        ALLELUIA!
  Shall the true Messiah see.

351

1 O'ER the distant mountains breaking,
  Comes the reddening dawn of day;

Rise, my soul, from sleep awaking,
  Rise and sing and watch and pray;
    'Tis thy Saviour!
  On His bright returning way.

2 Nearer is my soul's salvation,
    Spent the night, the day at hand.
  Keep me in my lowly station,
    Watching for Thee, till I stand,
        O my Saviour!
  In Thy bright and promised land.
            JOHN S. B. MONSELL, 1863. *Abr.*

352 The world is very evil.

"Looking for the blessed hope and appearing of the glory of our great God and Saviour Jesus Christ."

7s & 6s, D.

Pearsall.

Lat. BERNARD OF MORLAIX, 1150.
Tr. JOHN M. NEALE, 1851. *Abr.*

ST. GALL, KATHOLISCHE GESANGBUCH, 1851.

1. THE world is ver - y e - vil, The times are wax-ing late; Be so - ber and keep vig - il; The Judge is at the gate. The Judge that comes in mer - cy, The Judge that comes with might, To ter - min - ate the e - vil, To di - a - dem the right.

2 Arise, arise good Christian,
　Let right to wrong succeed,
　Let penitential sorrow
　　To heavenly gladness lead—
　To light that has no evening,
　　That knows nor moon nor sun,
　The light so new and golden,
　　The light that is but one.

3 And now we fight the battle:
　But then shall wear the crown
　Of full and everlasting
　　And passionless renown,
　And He, whom now we trust in,
　　Shall then be seen and known,
　And they that know and see Him
　　Shall have Him for their own.

353 Watchman! tell us of the night.

7s, D.

JOHN BOWRING, 1825.

"*He shall declare unto you the things that are to come.*"

Leyden.

Ad. fr. LOUIS SPOHR, 1833.

1. WATCHMAN! tell us of the night, What its signs of prom-ise are? Trav-'ler o'er yon mount-ain's height See that glo-ry-beam-ing star. Watch-man, doth its beau-teous ray, Aught of hope or joy fore-tell? Trav-'ler, yes, it brings the day, Promised day of Is-ra-el.

2 Watchman, tell us of the night,
  Higher yet that star ascends.
Traveler, blessedness and light,
  Peace and truth its course portends.
Watchman, will its beams alone
  Gild the spot that gave them birth?
Traveler, ages are its own,
  And it bursts o'er all the Earth.

3 Watchman, tell us of the night,
  For the morning seems to dawn.
Traveler, darkness takes its flight,
  Doubt and terror are withdrawn.
Watchman, let thy wanderings cease
  Hie thee to thy quiet home.
Traveler, lo! the Prince of Peace,
  Lo! the Son of God is come.

The Second Coming.

354

Hark! the song of Jubilee.

"Seeing that ye look for these things, give diligence that ye may be found in peace."

7s, D.   **Parousia.**

JAMES MONTGOMERY, 1819, 1825.   MAX PIUTTI, 1881.

1. HARK!—the song of Ju-bi-lee, Loud as might-y thun-ders roar, Or the full-ness of the sea, When it breaks up-on the shore,—"Al-le-lu-ia! for the Lord God om-nip-o-tent shall reign!" Al-le-lu-ia! let the word Ech-o round the earth and main.

Copyright, 1881, by Biglow & Main.

2 "Alleluia!" Hark! The sound,
  From the depths unto the skies,
Wakes, above, beneath, around,
  All creation's harmonies!
See Jehovah's banners furled!
  Sheathed His sword! He speaks—'tis done,
And the kingdoms of this world
  Are the kingdoms of His Son.

3 He shall reign from pole to pole
  With illimitable sway.
He shall reign, when, like a scroll,
  Yonder heavens have passed away,
Then the end. Beneath His rod,
  Man's last enemy shall fall.
Alleluia!—Christ in God,
  God in Christ, is All in All.

355 Wake! awake; for night is flying!

8s, 9s, 6s & 4s, P.   *"The day is at hand."*   **"Wachet auf!"**

Ger. Phillip Nicolai, 1597.
Tr. Cath. Winkworth, 1862. Alt.

Phillip Nicolai, 1599.
Arr. Benj. C. Blodgett, 1865.

sf Maestoso.

1. { Wake! a-wake; for night is fly - ing! The watchmen on the heights are cry - ing!
Midnight's sol-emn hour is toll - ing! His cha - riot-wheels are near - er roll - ing!

A - wake, Je - ru - sa - lem at last! }
Come forth, ye vir-gins, night is past! } A - rise! with will-ing feet Go forth, the Bridegroom meet.

Al - le - lu - ia! Bear thro the night your ready light, Speed forth to join the marriage rite.

2 Zion hears the watchmen singing,
Her heart with sudden joy is springing,
She wakes,—she stands in glad array!
Lo! her Lord draws near all-glorious,—
The strong in grace, in truth victorious,—
Her Star is ris'n, her night is day!
All hail, Thou Joy and Crown!
God's Son, from Heaven come down!
Alleluia!
We answer, all, Thy blessèd call,
And follow to the banquet hall.

3 Hear Thy praise, O Lord, ascending
From tongues of men and angels, blending
With harp and lute and cymbal's tone.
By Thy pearly gates in wonder
We stand and swell the voice of thunder,
In choral bursts about Thy Throne.
What vision never brought,
What ear hath never caught,—
Alleluia!—
Is ours! with song we join the throng
To praise Thee ages all along.

Life Eternal.

356   ## The sands of time are wasting.

7s & 6s, D.   *" Thine eyes shall see the King in His beauty."*   **Rutherford.**

ANNIE R. COUSIN, 1857. *Abr.*   CHRISTIAN URBAN, *d.* 1845.
Har. EDWARD F. RIMBAULT, 1845.

1. THE sands of time are wast - ing. The dawn of Heav-en breaks. The sum - mer

morn I've sighed for, The fair, sweet morn a - wakes. Oh, dark hath been the mid - night:

But day-spring is at hand, And glo - ry, glo - ry dwell-eth In Im-man-uel's land.

2 With mercy and with judgment,
    My web of time He wove,
  And aye the dews of sorrow
    Were lustered with His love.
  I'll bless the hand that guided,
    I'll bless the heart that planned,
  When throned where glory dwelleth,
    In Immanuel's land.

3 The bride eyes not her garment,
    But her dear bridegroom's face;
  I will not gaze at glory,
    But on my King of Grace,—
  Not at the crown He giveth,
    But on His piercèd hand;
  The Lamb is all the glory
    Of Immanuel's land.

357   A pilgrim and a stranger.

7s & 6s, D.   *"Whither the tribes go up."*   St. Hilda.

Ger. Paul Gerhardt, 1667.
Tr. Jane Borthwick, 1862. *Abr.*

* Justin H. Knecht, 1792: "* Edward Husband, 1871:
* † * William Henry Walter, 1872.

1. A pil-grim and a stranger, I jour-ney here be-low; Far dis-tant is my coun-try, The home to which I go. Here I must toil and tra-vail, Oft wea-ry and op-prest: But there my God shall lead me To ev-er-last-ing rest.

2 It is a well-worn pathway;
Many have gone before,—
The holy saints and prophets,
The patriarchs of yore.
They trod the toilsome journey
In patience and in faith,
And them I fain would follow,
Like them in life and death.

3 With them my thoughts are dwelling,
'Tis there I long to be;
Come, Lord! and call Thy servant
To blessedness with Thee!
Come, bid my toils be ended,
Let all my wanderings cease.
Call from the wayside lodging
To the sweet home of peace!

358 Beyond the horizon's misty skirt.

8.8.8.6.   *" There shall be no more sea."*   Edelweiss.

M. W. S., 1890.   G. W. TORRANCE.

1. BE - YOND th' ho - ri - zon's mist - y skirt, Be-yond the mel - an - chol - y sea,

A cit - y ris - es, glo - ry - girt, In light's im - mens - i - ty.

2 Its radiant gates all open stand,
   Its countless throngs are passing fair,
And blithesome spirits, hand in hand,
   Go singing everywhere.

3 There is no sundown there, no night,
   No bitter cry of grief or pain;
No sin can mar that deep delight,
   Nor requiem sound again.

4 The holy host of shining ones
   Speed on the errands of the King,
And lift supreme, in perfect tones,
   A chant unwavering.

5 The blest of every tongue and clime
   Rejoice to tell those ways of Love,
Which led them thro the toils of Time
   To purity above.

6 And One is there, whom each one knows
   For mercies separate to each,
And each to all His mercy shows;
   For men shall angels teach.

7 Oh, white apparel! happy place!
   Oh, song of rapture! Light benign!
Peace for all pilgrims! Christ, in grace,
   Make Thy dear city mine.

8.8.8.6.   SECOND TUNE.   Elmhurst.

E. D. DEWETT.

359   Upward where the stars are burning.

8.8.7.8.8.7.   *"Thou art my Lord. I have no good beyond Thee."*   **Civitas Dei.**

HORATIUS BONAR, 1866. *Abr.*

JOHN BAPTISTE CALKIN, 1872.
Arr. HUBERT P. MAIN, 1880.

1. Up-ward where the stars are burning, Si - lent, si-lent in their turning, Round the never-chang-ing pole;

Up-ward where the sky is brightest, Upward where the blue is lightest, Lift I now my long-ing soul.

Copyright, 1880, by Biglow & Main.

2 Far beyond that arch of gladness,
  Far beyond these clouds of sadness,
    Are the many mansions fair.
  Far from pain and sin and folly,
  In that palace of the holy,
    I would find my mansion there!

360   There is a happy land.

8.8.7.8.8.7.   *"A joyous town."*   **Eden.**

ANDREW YOUNG, 1838.

SAMUEL SEB. WESLEY, 1864.

1. THERE is a hap-py land, Far, far a - way, Where saints and angels stand, Bright, bright as day.

Life Eternal.

O how they sweetly sing, Worthy is our Saviour King, Loud let His praises ring, Praise, praise for aye!

2 Come to that happy land,
  Come, come away:
Why will ye doubting stand?
  Why still delay?
Oh, we shall happy be,
When from sin and sorrow free!
Lord, we shall live with Thee!
  Blest, blest for aye.

3 Bright in that happy land
  Beams every eye,
Kept by a Father's hand
  Love cannot die.
Oh then to glory run,
Be a crown and kingdom won,
And bright above the sun
  We'll reign for aye.

361   When I can read my title clear.

C. M.   *"Such confidence have we thro Christ."*   **Mirfield.**

ISAAC WATTS, 1707.   ARTHUR COTTMAN, 1872. *Har.* and *Alt.* B. C. B.

1 WHEN I can read my title clear
  To mansions in the skies,
I bid farewell to every fear,
  And wipe my weeping eyes.

2 Should Earth against my soul engage,
  And hellish darts be hurled,
Then I can smile at Satan's rage,
  And face a frowning world.

3 Let cares like a wild deluge come,
  And storms of sorrow fall;
May I but safely reach my home,
  My God, my Heaven, my all!

4 There shall I bathe my weary soul
  In seas of heavenly rest,
And not a wave of trouble roll
  Across my peaceful breast.

Life Eternal.

362
The people of the Lord.

S. M.

"Peace be within thy walls."

THOMAS KELLY, 1820.

Marion.

ARTHUR H. MESSITER, 1883.

1. The peo-ple of the Lord Are on their way to Heav'n; There they ob-tain their great reward, The

prize will there be giv'n. Re-joice! Re-joice! Re-joice, give thanks and sing!

By especial permission of the author.

2 'T is conflict here below;
   'T is triumph there, and peace:
   On Earth we wrestle with the foe;
   In Heaven our conflicts cease.

3 T is gloom and darkness here;
   'T is light and joy above;
   There all is pure, and all is clear;
   There all is peace and love.

4 There rest shall follow toil,
   And ease succeed to care:
   The victors there divide the spoil;
   They sing and triumph there.

5 Then let us joyful sing;
   The conflict is not long:
   We hope in Heaven to praise our King
   In one eternal song!

363
Heavenward, still heavenward.

7s, 5s & 4s.

"I press on toward the goal unto the prize."

"Gott ist die Ruh'."

Ger. J. G. SCHÖNER, d. 1818.
Tr. HENRY MILLS, 1845. Abr.

JOHANN RUDOLPH AHLE, cir. 1660.

mf

1. { Heav - en - ward, still heav - en - ward, Urge thy lin-g'ring feet: }
  { What de - serves thy chief re - gard, On - ly there to meet,— } Not here be - low.

Life Eternal.

Earthly hon - ors are in vain, }
Raise, if thou would'st glory gain, } From Earth thy view.

2 Heavenward He points thine eye,
There to seek thy prize:
Not deprest, nor rais'd too high,
By Earth's vanities.
Her wealth is poor;
From the good that here is won,
Only what for Heav'n is done
Will long endure.

364   Light after darkness.

5s 4s & 6s, P.
    "Be of good cheer."
Orient.

Frances R. Havergal, 1871.
Alfred Legge, 1887.

1. Light aft - er dark - ness, Gain aft - er loss, Strength aft - er weak - ness, Crown aft - er cross;

Sweet aft - er bit - ter, Hope aft - er fears, Home aft - er wand'ring, Praise aft-er tears.

2 Sheaves after sowing,
Sun after rain,
Sight after mystery,
Peace after pain;
Joy after sorrow,
Calm after blast,
Rest after weariness,
Sweet rest at last.

3 Near after distant,
Gleam after gloom,
Love after loneliness,
Life after tomb,
After long agony,
Rapture of bliss,
Right was the pathway
Leading to this!

Life Eternal.

365 There is a land mine eye hath seen.

L. M. "*Show me, I pray Thee, Thy glory.*" **Starlight.**

GURDON ROBINS, Jr., 1843. JOHN B. DYKES, 1858.

1. THERE is a land mine eye hath seen, In vis-ions of en - rapt - ured thought,

So bright that all which spreads be - tween, Is with its ra - diant glo - ry fraught.

2 A land upon whose blissful shore
  There rests no shadow, falls no stain;
  There those who meet shall part no more,
  And those long parted meet again.

3 Its skies are not like earthly skies,
  With varying hues of shade and light;
  It hath no need of suns to rise,
  To dissipate the gloom of night.

4 There sweeps no desolating wind
  Across that calm, serene abode;
  The wanderer there a home may find
  Within the paradise of God.

366
1 LET me be with Thee where Thou art,
  My Saviour, my eternal Rest;
  Then only will this longing heart
  Be fully and for ever blest.

2 Let me be with Thee where Thou art.
  Thine unveiled glory to behold;
  Then only will this wandering heart
  Cease to be faithless, treacherous, cold.

3 Let me be with Thee where Thou art,
  Where spotless saints Thy name adore;
  Then only will this sinful heart
  Be evil and defiled no more.

3 Let me be with Thee where Thou art,
  Where none can die, where none remove,
  Where life nor death my soul can part
  From Thy blest presence and Thy love.

CHARLOTTE ELLIOTT, 1836.

367
1 O SWEET Jerusalem above,
  Dear motherland of all the free!
  My tongue and hand prefer thy love,
  And far from home remember thee.

Life Eternal.

2 How shall we sing Jehovah's praise
  In this strange land of Babylon?
  We can but broken music raise,
  Till our captivity is done.

3 But joys untold shall breathe and burn
  Thro Zion's blest and holy throngs,
  When all the ransomed shall return
  With shouts and everlasting songs!

M. W. S., 1890.

368   Safe home, safe home in port!

6.6.6.6.8.8.   *"They all escaped safe to the land."*   **Anchorage.**

Gk, JOSEPH OF THE STUDIUM, 850.
Tr. JOHN M. NEALE, 1862. *Abr.*
     ARTHUR S. SULLIVAN, 1872.

1. SAFE home, safe home in port! Rent cordage, shattered deck, Torn sails, provisions short, And only not a wreck:— But oh, the joy up-on the shore To tell our voy-age per - ils o'er!

2 The prize, the prize secure!
  The athlete nearly fell,
  Bare all he could endure,
  And bare not always well:
  But he may smile at troubles gone
  Who sets the victor-garland on!

3 No more the foe can harm!
  No more of leaguered camp,
  And cry of night alarm,
  And need of ready lamp;
  And yet how nearly had he failed,—
  How nearly had that foe prevailed!

4 The lamb is in the fold,
  In perfect safety penned,
  The lion once had hold,
  And thought to make an end:
  But one came by with wounded side,
  And for the sheep the Shepherd died.

5 The exile is at home!
  Oh, nights and days of tears!
  Oh, longings not to roam!
  Oh, sins and doubts and fears!
  What matters now grief's darkest day?
  God's hand hath wiped all tears away!

Life Eternal.

369　The Homeland! Oh the Homeland!

7s, 6s & 8s P.　　　*" Then is finished the mystery of God."*　　　　**Homeland.**
HUGH R. HAWEIS.　　　　　　　　　　　　　　ARTHUR S. SULLIVAN, 1882.

1. THE Home-land! Oh the Home-land! The land of souls free-born! No gloom-y night is

known there, But aye the fade-less morn; I'm sigh-ing for that coun-try, My heart is

ach-ing here, There is no pain in the Home-land, To which I'm draw-ing near.

2 My Lord is in the Homeland,
　With angels bright and fair;
No sinful thing nor evil,
　Can ever enter there;
The music of the ransomed
　Is ringing in mine ears,
And when I think of the Homeland,
　Mine eyes gush out with tears.

3 For loved ones in the Homeland,
　Are calling me away
To rest and peace unending,
　And life beyond decay.
No death is in the Homeland,
　No sorrow is above,
Christ bring us all to the Homeland
　Of His eternal love!

Life Eternal.

370 By that Cross where Day with darkness strove.

9.6.6.8.8. *"For all the Earth is mine."* **Christus Pastor.**

M. W. S., 1896. Conrad Kocher, 1828.

1. By that Cross where Day with dark-ness strove, Where death gave way to Love, Our hearts al-

le-giance bring, And ev - er own "THIS IS THE KING!" AL - LE - LU - IA! AL-LE - LU - IA!

2 O'er Earth's battle-cloud His rainbows shine,—
We conquer by that sign!
Time's long campaign shall cease,
And Christ lead home His host in peace.

3 They have trod the storms beneath their feet.
Along the palm-strewn street
Cherubic legions run,
And swells their shout—" *Well done! Well done!*"

4 Lift your heads, ye dazzling gates of light,
And rock ye walls of might!
Peal out, ye golden bells,
From all your pearly citadels!

5 When Thou comest, scarred and glorious King,
While war-worn armies sing,
In Thy triumphant name
Grant us to share that vast acclaim!

371   Hark! hark! my soul! angelic songs.

11s, 10s & 9.   *" He shall give His angels charge over thee."*   **Pilgrims.**

FREDERICK W. FABER, 1854. *Abr.*   HENRY SMART, 1868.

1. Hark! hark! my soul! an-gel-ic songs are swelling O'er Earth's green fields, and ocean's wave-beat shore!

How sweet the truth those blessèd strains are tell-ing Of that new life when sin shall be no more.

An-gels of Je - sus! An - gels of light! Sing - ing to wel - come the pil-grims of the night.

2 Onward we go; for still we hear them singing,
     " Come, weary souls, for Jesus bids you come,"
   And thro the dark, its echoes sweetly ringing,
     The music of the Gospel leads us home.
         Angels of Jesus, &c.

3 Far, far away, like bells at evening pealing,
     The voice of Jesus sounds o'er land and sea,
   And laden souls, by thousands meekly stealing,
     Kind Shepherd! turn their weary steps to Thee.
         Angels of Jesus, &c.

Life Eternal.

4 Angels, sing on! your faithful watches keeping,
  Sing us sweet fragments of the songs above,
  Till morning's joy shall end the night of weeping,
  And life's long shadows break in cloudless love!
    Angels of Jesus, &c.

372   Forever with the Lord.

S. M.   *" It was but a little that I past from them, but I found Him whom my soul loveth."*   **Gorton.**

JAMES MONTGOMERY, 1835. *Abr.*   LUDWIG VAN BEETHOVEN.

1. For - ev - er with the Lord! A - men,—so let it be! Life from the dead is

in that word, 'Tis im - mor - tal - i - ty. A - men, A - men, A - men, A - men.

2 Here in the body pent,
    Absent from Him I roam:
  Yet nightly pitch my moving tent
    A day's march nearer home.

3 I hear at morn and even,
    At noon and midnight hour,
  The choral harmonies of Heaven.
    Earth's Babel tongues o'erpower.

4 Ah! then my spirit faints
    To reach the land I love,
  The bright inheritance of saints,
    Jerusalem above.

5 Be Thou at my right hand,
    Then can I never fail,
  Uphold Thou me, and I shall stand;
    Fight, and I must prevail.

6 So when my latest breath
    Shall rend the veil in twain,
  By death I shall escape from death,
    And life eternal gain.

7 Knowing as I am known,
    How shall I love that word,
  And oft repeat before the throne,
    "For ever with the Lord!" *Amen.*

373 The roseate hues of early dawn.

C. M. D. *"When that which is perfect is come, that which is in part shall be done away."* Jerusalem.

CECIL F. ALEXANDER, 1853. *Abr.* 　　　　　　　　　　　:S:　　　　　　LOUIS SPOHR, 1835.

1. THE ros-eate hues of ear-ly dawn, The brightness of the day. The crimson of the sun-set
D. S.—Oh, for the Sun of Righteous-

sky, How fast they fade a - way!　　Oh, for the pearl-y gates of Heav'n Oh, for the gold-en floor!
ness, That set-teth nev-er - more!

FINE.　　　　　　　　　　　　D. S.

2 Oh, for a heart that never sins!
Oh, for a soul washed white!
Oh, for a voice to praise our King,
Nor weary day or night!

Oh, by Thy love and anguish, Lord!
Oh, by Thy life laid down,
Grant that we fall not from Thy grace,
Nor cast away our crown!

374 I'm but a stranger here.

"We will go along the King's highway; we will not turn aside to the right hand nor to the left."

6s & 4s.　　　　　　　　　　　　Saint's Rest.

THOMAS RAWSON TAYLOR, 1835.　　　　ARTHUR S. SULLIVAN, 1872.

1. I'M but a stran-ger here, Heav'n is my home. Earth is a des-ert drear, Heav'n is my home.

Life Eternal.

Dan - ger and sorrow stand Round me on ev-'ry hand; Heav'n is my Fa-ther-land, Heav'n is my home.

2 What tho the tempest rage,
  Heaven is my home.
 Short is my pilgrimage,
  Heaven is my home.
 Time's wild and wintry blast
 Soon will be overpast,
 I shall reach home at last;
  Heaven is my home.

3 There, at my Saviour's side,—
  Heaven is my home!
 I shall be glorified;—
  Heaven is my home.
 There are the good and blest,
 Those I love most and blest,
 There too I soon shall rest;
  Heaven is my home.

375   Sing Alleluia forth in duteous praise.

10.10.7.   "And they shall see His face."   **Alleluia Perenne.**
Lat. 5th Cent. *Tr.* JOHN ELLERTON, 1868. *Abr.*   WILLIAM H. MONK, 1868.

1. SING Al-le - lu - ia forth in duteous praise, Ye citizens of Heav'n; Oh, sweetly raise An endless Alleluia.   A - MEN.

2 Ye Powers who stand before th' Eternal Light,
  In hymning choirs re-echo to the height an endless Alleluia.

3 The Holy City shall take up your strain,
  And with glad songs resounding wake again an endless Alleluia.

4 Ye who have gained at length your palms in bliss,
  Victorious ones, your chant shall still be this, an endless Alleluia.

5 There, in one grand acclaim, for ever ring
  The strains which tell the honor of your King, an endless Alleluia.

376   Eternal day hath owned the Prince of Life.

P. M.   "*Before the presence of His glory, without blemish.*"   **Amaranth.**

M. W. S., 1881.   *Ad. fr.* GIOACCHINO A. ROSSINI, 1823.

Andante.

1. E - TER - NAL day hath owned The Prince of Life enthroned! Thro gates of am - e - thyst, To
2. These that con-fest the Name, These that de-spised the shame,—They walk with Him in white; For

the great en - chan - rist, The Church of Christ,—Purchase of love un-priced! Streams in, a
well they fought the fight. Kept they the faith, Won mor-tal sor-row's graith; Now by Im-

ransom'd throng, Up-lift-ing end-less song. Each brow one Name doth gem, Brighter than di - a - dem.
man-uel's grace, Transform'd beneath His face, Long as E - ter - ni - ty, The bless - ed One they see!

Copyright, 1881, by Biglow & Main.

3 God hath wiped every tear,
  Ended all doubt and fear,
  Crying and pain are o'er,
  And death shall be no more.
    All things are new!
  Faithful for aye and True,
  The King of kings hath come,
  Fetch'd all His banished home,
  Jesus hath kept His word,
  The Bride is with her Lord.

4 Perfected peace at last!
  Earth's tribulation past.
  There is no longer night;
  The Lamb doth give them light.
    Every whit whole
  Each new-born ransomed soul!
  For every heart athirst
  Celestial fountains burst.
  Along the heavenly meads
  His flock their Shepherd leads.

377   Jerusalem, the golden.

"The voice of joy, and the voice of gladness, the voice of the Bridegroom, and the voice of the Bride, the voice of them that shall say, Praise the Lord of hosts; for the Lord is good; for His mercy endureth forever."

7s & 6s, D.   **Ewing.**

Lat. BERNARD OF MORLAIX, 1150.   ALEXANDER EWING, 1853.
Tr. JOHN M. NEALE, 1851.

1. Je - ru - sa - lem, the gold - en, With milk and hon - ey blest! Be-neath thy contem-pla - tion Sink heart and voice op - prest. I know not, oh, I know not What so-cial joys are there! What ra - dian - cy of glo - ry, What light beyond com-pare!

2 There grief is turned to pleasure;
  Such pleasure as below
No human voice can utter,
  No human heart can know.
And after fleshly scandal,
  And after this world's night,
And after storm and whirlwind,
  Is calm and joy and light.

3 There is the throne of David!
  And there, from care released,
The song of them that triumph,
  The shout of them that feast.
And they, who with their Leader,
  Have conquered in the fight,
For ever and for ever
  Are clad in robes of white!

378 Praise we the Father with exulting voices.

"Thine be the Kingdom, the power, and the glory forever, Amen."

11.11.11.10.
FANNY J. CROSBY, 1896.

Carmen Eternitatis.
HUBERT P. MAIN, 1896.

1. PRAISE we the Fa-ther with ex-ult-ing voic - es, Him in whose mercy world on world re - joic - es,

Thronging be - fore Him, wor- ship and a - dore Him;—Glo-ry and hon - or to His ho - ly name!

2 Praise we the Saviour. By that incarnation,
Lowly and mighty,—Love's own revelation,
Join we the raptured choral of Creation;—
Loud alleluias to His holy name!

3 Power of the Highest, all Thy pilgrims guiding,
In truth and beauty steadfastly presiding,
Kindly and gently in our hearts abiding,
Laud and thanksgiving to Thy holy name!

4 Praise for that birthright which we now inherit,—
Life everlasting, thro one only Merit,—
Lord God eternal, Father Son, and Spirit,
Glory and honor to Thy holy name!

5 In Heaven's high music, all its floods upflinging
In one sweet storm,—all saints and angels singing,
Let us, unworthy, boundless anthems bringing,
Praise and forever bless Thy holy name.

978-3-33730-511-6

Indian life and Indian history is an unchanged, high-quality reprint of the original edition of 1860.
Hansebooks is editor of the literature on different topic areas such as research and science, travel and expeditions, cooking and nutrition, medicine, and other genres. As a publisher we focus on the preservation of historical literature. Many works of historical writers and scientists are available today as antiques only. Hansebooks newly publishes these books and contributes to the preservation of literature which has become rare and historical knowledge for the future.

ISBN/EAN: 978-3-33730-511-6
www.hansebooks.com

hanse

INDEX OF AUTHORS AND COMPOSERS.

"Such as found out musical tunes, and recited verses in writing."

261

ALPHABETICAL INDEX OF TUNES.

INDEX OF FIRST LINES.